Better Homes and Gardens®

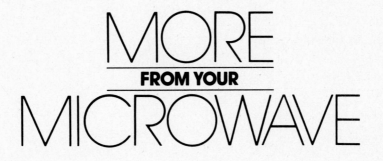

© 1980 by Meredith Corporation, Des Moines, Iowa.
All Rights Reserved. Printed in the United States of America.
First Edition. First Printing.
Library of Congress Catalog Card Number: 79-93395
ISBN: 0-696-00615-4

BETTER HOMES AND GARDENS® BOOKS

Editor: Gerald M. Knox
Art Director: Ernest Shelton

Food and Nutrition Editor: Doris Eby
Senior Food Editor: Sharyl Heiken
Senior-Associate Food Editors: Sandra Granseth,
    Elizabeth Woolever
Associate Food Editors: Bonnie Lasater,
    Marcia Stanley, Joy Taylor, Pat Teberg,
    Diana Tryon
Recipe Development Editor: Marion Viall
Test Kitchen Director: Sharon Golbert
Test Kitchen Home Economists: Jean Brekke,
    Kay Cargill, Marilyn Cornelius, Maryellyn Krantz,
    Marge Steenson

Associate Art Directors: Neoma Alt West,
    Randall Yontz
Copy and Production Editors: David Kirchner,
    Lamont Olson, David Walsh
Assistant Art Director: Harijs Priekulis
Senior Graphic Designer: Faith Berven
Graphic Designers: Linda Ford,
    Sheryl Veenschoten, Tom Wegner

Editor-in-Chief: James A. Autry
Editorial Director: Neil Kuehnl
Group Administrative Editor: Duane Gregg
Executive Art Director: William J. Yates

MORE FROM YOUR MICROWAVE
Editor: Sharyl Heiken
Consultant: Cy DeCosse Creative Department, Inc.
Copy and Production Editor: David Kirchner

Our seal assures you that every recipe in
More From Your Microwave is endorsed by
the Better Homes and Gardens Test Kitchen.
Each recipe is tested for family appeal,
practicality, and deliciousness.

CONTENTS

What are Microwaves?

Microwaves are non-ionizing electromagnetic waves. This common form of energy surrounds us all the time. It includes visible light from the sun or an ordinary light bulb, infrared waves from your fireplace, and radio waves, as well as microwaves.

Don't confuse this form of energy with ionizing waves, such as X rays or ultraviolet rays. Visible light, radio waves, and microwaves do not have the same strength or effect as ionizing waves.

HOW MICROWAVES WORK

Microwave energy diminishes rapidly. Microwaves lose 99 percent of their energy within 10 inches from their source. In order to cook, they must be enclosed in a small space. Since microwaves cannot penetrate metal, a metal box is used to contain them.

The microwave alternates between positive and negative directions, and acts like a magnet on the positive and negative particles in food molecules, especially water, fat, and sugar molecules.

The microwave field changes direction nearly 2½ billion times a second, so the food molecules vibrate at the same speed. Friction between molecules produces heat in the food, causing it to cook.

HOW FOODS COOK

It's a myth that microwaves cook from the inside out. Microwaves penetrate foods to a depth of ¾ to 1½ inches on all surfaces: top, bottom, and sides. They cause no chemical change in the food, but they do generate heat in the areas penetrated. From there, the heat spreads by conduction to the center of the food, just as it does in conventional cooking. Some of the heat also spreads to the surface and is lost in the surrounding air.

A few foods that have a high sugar content and that are thin enough for the microwaves to penetrate to the center may become hotter on the inside. One example is a marshmallow. If it is overheated, the center may burn while the surface appears normal because it has lost some heat to the air. A jelly-filled roll may feel warm on the outside but be very hot in the center, because sugary jelly attracts more microwave energy than the porous bread.

MICROWAVE OVENS ARE SAFE

The metal box that encloses the microwaves so they can cook also keeps the energy safely inside the oven. Federal law requires that ovens be designed so that they cannot operate with the door open. Two independent interlock systems prevent transmission of energy when the door is not securely fastened. A monitoring system assures that the oven will not work if the interlock systems fail.

Before it leaves the manufacturer, every oven must be tested to make sure it meets very strict government safety standards. It is tested for possible leakage of microwave energy within 2 inches of the oven door. You can be certain that any oven that is safe at 2 inches is definitely safe at operating distance.

A Miniature Broadcasting System

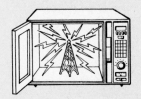

The microwave oven is a miniature self-contained radio broadcasting system. The microwave signal is broadcast by the magnetron and is converted to heat in food, just as a radio signal is converted to sound in your radio.

The photo at left was taken through the oven door as a fresh pear micro-cooked in a bubbling syrup flavored with brandy and spices. The air in the oven remained cool.

Variable Power Levels

The first microwave ovens offered only one power level; they were either on or off. Microwave cooking was limited to those foods that cook well at High or Full power.

Many of our most popular foods do cook well at High power, but the older microwave ovens couldn't prepare tougher cuts of meat or delicate egg dishes. Defrosting was fast, but it took a lot of attention to make sure parts of the food didn't start to cook while the rest was still solidly frozen. The introduction of variable power microwave ovens made microwave cooking versatile and flexible.

HOW VARIABLE POWER WORKS

Microwave ovens with variable power automatically cycle energy on and off. Short pulses of energy alternate with periods of no energy. These rest periods help equalize the internal temperature of the food, and allow you to cook foods like pot roast, eggs, and cream, which are sensitive to high concentrations of energy.

The lower power levels are preset to provide a percentage of the oven's full power. Most of today's microwave ovens have at least two settings, High and Defrost. The Defrost setting may be 30 percent to 50 percent of the oven's full power, depending upon the make of oven, and can be used for cooking as well as defrosting.

Other microwave ovens have three to six settings. The name and power assigned to each setting vary with the make and model. On ovens with ten settings, the numbers correspond to the percentage of power. A setting of 5 indicates 50 percent of full power.

MICROWAVING SAVES ENERGY

Most of us know that microwaving consumes less energy than conventional cooking. Foods cook faster, and energy heats the food directly, rather than the pan or the air around it. Actual savings vary with the amount and type of food cooked.

Variable power microwave ovens save energy, too. Although it takes twice as long to cook a food at 50 percent of power, it takes exactly the same amount of energy. If you are used to microwave speed at High power, the 1 to 1½ hours needed to microwave a pot roast at Medium power may seem long, but remember that it would take 3 to 4 hours to cook the same roast conventionally.

TERMS USED IN THIS BOOK

When variable power ovens were introduced, some manufacturers named the different settings after familiar cooking terms, such as "roast" or "bake," while others used the terms "Medium-High" or "Low," which were similar to heat settings associated with range-top cooking. It soon became evident that consumers needed a standard terminology so they could make use of new cook books, magazine articles, and recipes collected from friends.

How to Use Variable Power

Conventional range burners can be turned up or down to control the amount of heat transmitted to food.

Variable power microwave ovens cycle energy on and off to give you the same control and flexibility. If a fruit pie or sauce bubbles too hard on 100% (HIGH), reduce the power by one setting. If a large batch of chili will not hold a simmer on 50% (MEDIUM), increase power to 60 or 70%.

A panel representing manufacturers and consumers met to determine which percentages of power were used most frequently and which terms would be most meaningful to consumers. The resulting standard percentages and terms, shown in the chart at right, are based on ovens with 600 to 650 watts.

There are also small-cavity counter top microwave ovens of 575 watts, and large-cavity ovens that exceed 650 watts. Because cavity size is adjusted, cooking in these ovens is comparable to standard counter top ovens of 600 to 650 watts.

HOW TO TEST YOUR OVEN FOR A MEDIUM SETTING

Most recipes in this book call for a High setting of 100 percent of power or a Medium setting of 50 percent of power. On some microwave ovens, the setting labeled Medium may be as high as 70 percent, while the defrost setting on a two-power oven may be 40 percent or 30 percent. To check a setting, use this test.

You will need a clock with a second hand, a 4-cup measure, and a 1-cup measure. Combine 1 cup of cold tap water and 8 ice cubes in the 4-cup measure. Stir for 1 minute. Pour off 1 cup of water into the 1-cup measure and discard the ice cubes and remaining water.

Micro-cook the water at High until it reaches a full boil. This should take 3 to 4 minutes. Time it carefully and record the time. Discard the hot water and let both measuring cups return to room temperature.

Repeat the experiment with fresh water and ice cubes, using the lower setting you wish to test. If the water takes approximately twice as long to boil, the setting is 50 percent of power, and corresponds to the Medium setting used in this book.

If the water boils in less than twice the time, the setting is higher than 50 percent, and a lower setting probably corresponds to Medium. If the defrost setting on a two-power oven takes more than twice the time, you can still use it to cook recipes that call for Medium power, but it will take the maximum time or a little longer.

CONVENIENCE FOODS AND VARIABLE POWER

Many convenience foods now carry microwave directions on the package. Most of them are for High power, although a few frozen foods include instructions for using lower power settings.

Even when directions are for High power, a combination of High and Medium will give you better results, especially with 10- to 12-ounce frozen entrées and foods that cannot be stirred, such as salisbury steak, lasagne, veal parmesan, or vegetable soufflés.

To take advantage of variable power, micro-cook the food at High for 1/3 of the total time recommended in the food manufacturer's directions. This gets defrosting started and breaks down ice crystals. Now reduce the power setting to Medium. Micro-cook for the remaining time, *plus* 1/3 more time.

Power Level Chart

This chart shows the standard terms and the approximate percentage of power assigned to each setting.

SETTING	%
High	100%
Medium-High	70%
Medium	50%
Medium-Low	30%
Low	10%

Recipe Timing

All brands of microwave ovens do not cook at the same speed. Even the same oven may be very fast at one time of day, but cook more slowly during periods of peak power consumption. The recipes in this book provide time spans broad enough to allow for these differences. Always check food after the minimum time, then continue microwaving until it is cooked to your satisfaction.

Techniques at a Glance

Cover to speed cooking.

Stir to distribute heat.

Turn over large pieces.

Arrange dishes or food in a ring with thin parts to center, or center empty.

Shield with pieces of foil to prevent overcooking.

Rotate foods that cannot be stirred.

Let stand to complete cooking and to develop flavor.

Microwave Techniques

Many microwave cooking techniques are familiar to you from conventional cooking. Others are unique to microwaving. All of them speed cooking and equalize heat to help the food cook evenly.

Since microwaves penetrate the surfaces of food, the outside areas absorb more energy than the center. In many microwave ovens, some parts of the cavity receive more energy than others. By using techniques that equalize heat, you can make sure that all parts of the food are done at the same time.

Covering. Microwaving is a moist cooking method. Although most foods will not dry out, using a cover holds in steam and helps food cook faster. Covering food gives you the full benefit of microwave speed.

Stirring. This is one of the most useful microwave cooking techniques. Stirring food from the outside to the center of the dish redistributes heat. You don't need to stir as often as you would conventionally; several times during cooking is usually sufficient unless your oven has a very uneven heating pattern.

Turning over or rearranging. Since parts of the oven cavity receive less energy than others, turning over or rearranging large items, such as whole vegetables and pieces of meat, moves them into a new energy pattern and helps all parts cook evenly.

Arranging in the oven. It's natural to place a single item in the center of the oven, but when you are cooking several pieces at the same time, arrange them in a ring. Keep space between them, and leave the center open so energy can penetrate from all sides.

Arranging in the dish. Take advantage of the fact that the center of a dish receives less energy than the outside. Arrange the food so that thin or delicate parts, such as the tails of fish fillets or the tips of asparagus spears, are in the center, with thick or tough parts near the outside.

Shielding. This technique protects areas that absorb the most energy so the rest of the food can catch up. The most common method is to use strips of foil to shield the top of a large roast, the wing tips of poultry, or the ends of a loaf dish. Another form of shielding is to cover meat with a sauce or vegetables.

Rotating. Some foods, such as cake or lasagne, cannot be stirred during cooking. Giving the dish a quarter- or half-turn will bring the food into a new energy pattern, and help it heat evenly.

STANDING TIME

Standing time is probably the most important of all cooking techniques, but it takes place *after* microwaving. By allowing foods to stand, you make sure that they are fully cooked but not overcooked. Even conventionally, foods continue to cook after they are removed from the heat, but this is far more noticeable with microwaved foods. They build up such high internal heat that they can finish cooking outside the oven. Large or dense foods need the most standing time. If you microwave a potato until the center is soft, the outside will be mushy. When you are planning a meal, allow enough time for foods that need to stand. Use that time to microwave another food.

Recipe Conversion

As you become familiar with microwave recipes, you'll notice that many of the foods are similar to ones you cook conventionally. In fact, about 80 to 90 percent of the foods you cook conventionally can be prepared in your microwave oven.

Which recipes to convert. Microwaving is a moist cooking method. The easiest foods to microwave are those that are naturally moist, such as chicken, fish, ground beef, vegetables, and fruits. Other good choices are saucy main dishes and casseroles, and foods that are steamed, covered, or stirred during cooking.

Microwaved foods do not develop a dry, crisp crust. If this is an important feature of your recipe, you should probably cook it conventionally. Microwaved casseroles can be given a crisp, brown surface by adding a topping after the final stirring.

Find a similar microwave recipe. Your best guide for recipe conversion is a microwave cook book. Look for a microwave recipe that starts with the same amount and type of main solid ingredient as your conventional recipe. For example, if you want to convert a meat loaf using 1½ pounds of ground beef, find a microwave recipe that calls for the same amount of meat. Use the microwave recipe as a guide to selecting a utensil, power level, cooking technique, and time.

WHAT TO CHANGE

Some recipes need no changes, other than a microwave cooking dish and less cooking time. Others require slight changes in the amounts of some ingredients due to the way microwaves cook.

Fats. Many conventional recipes call for fat to keep foods from sticking to the pan. With microwaving, you can eliminate fats or add just a tablespoon of butter, margarine, or olive oil for flavor.

Liquids. Microwaved foods retain their moisture and usually cook so rapidly that little evaporation occurs. When you convert a conventional recipe, reduce the liquid by about ⅓. Check frequently during cooking, and add more liquid if the food appears dry.

Seasonings. Microwaving brings out the natural flavor of food, so you may not want as much seasoning. Small amounts of herbs and spices need not be changed, but use slightly less salt and pepper. After microwaving, adjust the seasoning to taste.

TIMING

The greatest change will occur in cooking time. Your best guide is a similar microwave recipe, but if you can't find one, try cutting the conventional time to ⅓ or ¼. Test for doneness frequently. If the food needs more cooking time, add it in small amounts.

How to Increase or Decrease Quantity

Microwave cooking times depend on the amount and depth of food in the dish. If you change the number of servings, you must change the time, too. Use a dish that is deep enough to prevent boilovers and wide enough to keep the depth of food the same as in the original recipe.

Decrease time by ⅓ when you halve a microwave recipe. To double a recipe, add ½ to ⅔ more microwave time.

Dish Test

If you are not certain that a glass, pottery, or china dish is microwave-safe, use this test. Pour ½ cup cold water into a glass measure. Set it inside or beside the dish you wish to test. Micro-cook 1 minute at High.

If the water is warm but the dish remains cool, the dish can be used for cooking. If the water is warm and the dish feels lukewarm, the dish is suitable for heating or reheating food.

If the water stays cool while the dish becomes hot, do not use the dish in your microwave oven for any purpose.

This test is not satisfactory for plastic containers, since most plastics are transparent to microwaves. Distortion of some plastics is due to contact with hot food, not microwave energy.

Microwave Utensils

With more and more households cooking with microwaves, the microwave utensil industry is growing. In addition to items designed for microwaving, many conventional utensils are suitable, too, including some things you may not have thought of as cookware.

You may have heard that microwave utensils don't get hot; this is not true. The ideal utensil is transparent to microwaves; it allows the energy to pass through the container and heat the food. However, once the food becomes hot, some heat is transferred to the dish. Some materials that are excellent for heating foods should not be used for cooking. Select the right utensil for each job.

PAPER

Paper toweling, plates, and cups. These are convenient for heating foods, and for cooking up to 4 minutes on High. White paper products are safest, since some colored dyes may bleed or be toxic. If you are heating a beverage, be sure to use a hot drink cup. Select plastic-coated plates for heating and serving moist foods, and non-coated paper plates to absorb moisture with sandwiches, crackers, or dry and crisp foods.

Paper baking cups. These not only reduce cleanup, but they absorb excess moisture when you microwave cupcakes and muffins. Don't use them with recipes containing very high amounts of sugar and fat because they may catch fire.

Ovenable paper. These containers are designed for use in both microwave and conventional ovens. Since they withstand oven temperatures up to 400°, they can be used to microwave any foods that are also recommended for conventional oven cooking.

Waxed paper. Paraffin is transparent to microwaves, so the wax will not melt unless it comes in contact with very hot food. Use waxed paper as a cover to prevent spatters or when you want to hold in heat for faster cooking, yet allow some steam to escape.

OVEN GLASS AND GLASS-CERAMIC

These are among the most useful microwave utensils. You may already have many of them for conventional cooking. With a microwave oven, you can measure, mix, and cook in one oven glass measuring cup. Clear glass baking dishes allow you to check for doneness on the bottom of cakes, pies, and breads.

POTTERY AND CHINA

Many plates and serving dishes make good microwave utensils. If you are cooking in them, be sure the dish can withstand high temperatures. Porcelain and stoneware are good choices because they are usually conventional oven-proof, too. Don't use a dish with gold or silver trim or a signature on the bottom. The metal may blacken or overheat the area next to it and crack the dish.

PLASTICS

Most plastics, except Melamine®, are transparent to microwaves, but vary in the food temperatures they can withstand. Some that are suitable for heating will melt or distort during cooking. When you buy a utensil labeled "microwave-safe" or "suitable for microwaving," read the manufacturer's directions carefully, and use the dish only for the types of foods recommended.

Styrofoam®. Containers made of Styrofoam® are suitable for heating foods to serving temperature, but begin to distort at 170°.

Storage and tableware plastics. Most of these can be used for heating foods to a normal serving temperature of 140°. They distort at fairly low temperatures, so they should not be used for cooking or for heating foods high in fat or sugar content.

Polysulfone and thermo-set-filled polyesters. These plastics withstand temperatures from 325° to 425°, and can be used in a conventional oven, too. Follow the manufacturer's recommendations for the types of food to cook in each utensil.

METAL

Most newer microwave ovens are designed to prevent energy feedback to the magnetron and permit some use of metal. Read the manufacturer's warranty, and do not use metal if it is prohibited.

Metal reflects microwave energy so it can't penetrate the food. The reflective properties of metal can be used to advantage. During defrosting, you can "shield" areas that defrost early. Without shielding, areas that were already thawed would start to cook while the rest of the food was still frozen. During cooking, shields protect parts of the food that tend to overcook, such as the corners of brownies and poultry wing tips.

Frozen entrees in shallow foil pans will heat evenly from the top only, without overcooking the corners and sides. If the lid is foil-lined, you must remove it or the food will receive no energy at all.

The amount of metal used must be in proportion to the amount of food. A foil tray should be ⅔ to ¾ full. Metal sometimes reflects energy onto the material around it. Thus, the clamps used to secure turkey legs can be left in during defrosting, but should be removed before cooking. Metal twist ties on plastic bags should always be replaced with string or a strip of plastic, since energy reflected from the wire tie could cause the plastic to melt.

COVERS

If your casserole has a glass or pottery lid, you can use it in the microwave. A sheet of waxed paper acts like a "partial cover." It holds in heat but allows some steam to escape.

If your dish has no cover, non-stretch clear plastic wrap is excellent, but it must be vented to prevent buildup of excess steam pressure, which can split the plastic. To vent, cover the dish with plastic wrap, then fold it back along one edge to make a 2-inch-long slot between the wrap and the rim of the dish.

Special Accessories

***Browning utensils** of glass-ceramic are available in several sizes and styles. A special coating on the bottom absorbs microwave energy. After it is preheated, the dish sears, browns, or grills foods. The utensil is raised on legs so the hot bottom will not mar counter tops.*

***Probes and thermometers** help you judge doneness by temperature. Microwave meat and candy thermometers work like the conventional thermometers, which cannot be used in a microwave oven. Probes are standard equipment on many ovens. When the food reaches a preset internal temperature, the probe turns the oven off or switches to a keep-warm setting automatically.*

Four Steps To A Microwave Meal

1. *Prepare foods that are to be served chilled or at room temperature, or that can be reheated later.*

2. *Cook foods with long standing or holding times and set aside.*

3. *Microwave quick-cooking foods, or reheat dishes made in advance.*

4. *Warm last-minute foods, such as rolls or pies.*

Menu Planning

The secret of microwaving a whole meal is good time management. When you plan and prepare a meal, take advantage of these four characteristics of microwave cooking.

Standing time is needed to finish cooking many foods. Allow for it in your plan and use the time to prepare another food.

Holding time is the length of time a micro-cooked food will stay hot if properly covered or wrapped. Most casseroles and medium-size meats and vegetables retain their heat 10 to 20 minutes beyond the standing time. After standing, large, dense roasts and vegetables can be held an additional 20 to 45 minutes.

Reheating foods in a microwave oven restores their fresh-cooked flavor.

Quick-cooking foods can be microwaved at the last minute. Remember that while one food is in the oven, you can get another ready to cook. You also can combine microwave and conventional cooking. For example, micro-cook spaghetti sauce in the time it takes to boil water and cook pasta conventionally.

SUNDAY DINNER

Chicken Parmesan, page 49
Italian Medley, page 81
Tossed Green Salad
French Bread
Individual Custards, page 89

Micro-cook custards first, then Chicken Parmesan. Let chicken stand while micro-cooking Italian Medley and tossing salad.

FAMILY SUPPER

Sauced Meat Loaf, page 31
Baked Potatoes, page 85
Carrots, page 84
Cole Slaw
Chocolate Chip Bars, page 90

Prepare and refrigerate Cole Slaw while micro-cooking Chocolate Chip Bars. Micro-cook Baked Potatoes. Wrap in foil; let stand. Micro-cook Sauced Meat Loaf. Let stand while cooking Carrots.

COMPANY ROAST

Hawaiian Pork Roast, page 36
Hot Cooked Rice
Peas, Onion, Mushrooms, and Almonds, page 81
Blueberry Cheesecake, page 91

Early in the day, prepare and refrigerate Blueberry Cheesecake. Cook rice conventionally while micro-cooking Hawaiian Pork Roast. While roast stands, micro-cook Peas, Onion, Mushrooms, and Almonds.

Reheating

The microwave oven reheats foods without loss of flavor or texture. Whether you make a dish in advance or are serving leftovers, the food will be fresh-tasting. Most foods are reheated from a refrigerated state. If you prepare food an hour or two before serving time and let it stand at room temperature, reduce the reheating time. Stir or rotate food as you would during cooking. Use a 50% (*MEDIUM*) setting for sliced meats and large amounts of casseroles or main dishes that cannot be stirred. A good way to test plates of food is to feel the bottom of the dish, especially in the center. When the food is hot enough to warm the dish, it's ready.

Food and Amount	Power Level	Time	Method
Chicken Pieces			
1 piece	100% (HIGH)	1½-3½ min.	Cover with waxed paper.
2 pieces	100% (HIGH)	2½-4½ min.	
Chops, Ribs			
1 serving	100% (HIGH)	1½-3 min.	Cover with waxed paper.
2 servings	100% (HIGH)	2½-4½ min.	
Hamburgers, Meat Loaf *(4-ounce serving)*			
1 serving	100% (HIGH)	30-60 sec.	Cover with waxed paper.
2 servings	100% (HIGH)	¾-1¾ min.	
Thinly Sliced Roast Meats *(4-ounce serving)*			
1 or more servings	50% (MEDIUM)	45-60 sec. per serving	Top slices with gravy. Cover with waxed paper. When heating several servings, check after 30 seconds per serving and rotate dish.
Frankfurters			
1 frankfurter	100% (HIGH)	15-30 sec.	When reheating in bun, wrap in a paper towel to prevent bun from getting soggy.
2 frankfurters	100% (HIGH)	30-60 sec.	
Main Dishes, Casseroles *(1 cup per serving)*			
1 serving	100% (HIGH)	1½-3½ min.	Cover saucy dishes with vented clear plastic wrap. Cover others with waxed paper. Stir or rotate after ½ of time.
2 servings	100% (HIGH)	2-4½ min.	
3 servings	100% (HIGH)	5-9 min.	

Defrosting

All variable-power ovens have a defrost setting, which may be from 30 percent to 50 percent of power. If you are defrosting on 100% (*HIGH*), follow the directions in your microwave oven manual. The following chart gives times on a 50% (*MEDIUM*) setting for foods taken from a freestanding freezer at 0°F. If your oven has a defrost setting of less than 50 percent power, you may need to increase the timings. If you store foods in a refrigerator-freezer, you may need to reduce the timings, since the temperature of most freezer compartments is usually 15° to 20°F.

Food	Power Level	Time	Let Stand After Defrosting	Method
Ground Beef, Lamb, or Pork 1 pound	50%	3¾-5 min.	5 min.	Turn over after first ⅓ of time. Break up meat and remove soft pieces after second ⅓ of time.
Ground Beef Patty 1 patty 2 patties	50% 50%	3¾-5 min. 3¾-5 min.	3-5 min. 3-5 min.	Turn over and rearrange after ½ of time.
Flat Roasts and Large Steaks	50%	3-5 min. per pound	5 min.	Defrost in microwave-oven-safe package for ½ of time. Unwrap. Shield warm areas with foil. Turn meat over and place in baking dish.
Large Roasts	50%	5-7 min. per pound	15-25 min. or until a skewer can be inserted into center of roast	Defrost in microwave-oven-safe package for ¼ of time. Unwrap. Shield warm areas with foil. Turn meat over and place in baking dish. Let stand 10 minutes after second ¼ of time. Shield and turn over after third ¼ of time.
Chops and Small Steaks	50%	3-4 min. per pound	3-5 min.	Defrost in microwave-oven-safe package for ½ of time. Separate pieces. Place in baking dish with least-defrosted parts to outside.
Cubed Meats	50%	3-4 min. per pound	5 min.	Defrost in microwave-oven-safe package for ½ of time. Unwrap. Separate cubes and place in baking dish. Remove any thawed pieces.
Whole Chicken	50%	3-6 min. per pound	5 min.	Turn after ½ of time, remove giblets, and rinse well.
Cut-Up Chicken Pieces	50%	2½-5 min. per pound	5 min.	Separate and rearrange pieces after ½ of defrosting time.
Chicken Quarters	50%	4-6 min. per pound	5 min.	Separate and rearrange after ⅓ of time. Rearrange again after ⅔ of time.

Food packaged in paper or plastic can be placed in the oven without unwrapping. Remove packaging as soon as possible to speed defrosting. Cover food with waxed paper to hold in heat.

For even defrosting, break up or separate pieces after the first ⅓ to ½ of defrosting time. Remove any thawed portions so they will not start to cook. Turn over large items several times, and shield any areas that feel warm. Let bulky foods stand 10 to 20 minutes to complete defrosting. When thawed, food should feel cool, but can be pierced to the center with a skewer.

Food	Power Level	Time	Let Stand After Defrosting	Method
Boneless Chicken Breasts	50%	5-8 min. per pound	5 min.	Rearrange after ⅓ of time; turn over after ⅔ of time.
Whole Turkey	50%	3½-5½ min. per pound	20-30 min. in cool water or until giblets can be removed	Defrost breast side down ¼ of time; shield warm areas with foil and turn breast side up. Defrost second ¼ of time. Shield warm areas if needed; turn turkey over and rotate dish. Defrost third ¼ of time; turn turkey over. Defrost last ¼ of time or until wings and legs can be separated from body.
Turkey Parts	50%	3-6 min. per pound	5-10 min. or till fork can pierce	Defrost ½ of time; turn parts over and re-arrange. Defrost remaining time. Rinse under cool water.
Turkey Breast	50%	3½-5 min. per pound	5-10 min. or until fork can pierce thickest part	Place meatiest side down; defrost ½ of time. Shield warm spots; turn meatiest side up. Defrost remaining time. Rinse under cool water.
Cornish Game Hens	50%	5-7 min. per pound	5-10 min.	Unwrap. Place breast side down. Cover with waxed paper. Defrost ½ of time; turn breast side up. Defrost remaining time.
Fish Fillets 1 pound	50%	3-5 min. per pound	5 min.	Separate fillets and rearrange after ⅓ of time; rearrange after ⅔ of time.
Fish Steaks	50%	3-5 min. per pound	5-6 min.	Separate and rearrange after ½ of time.
Small Whole Fish	50%	3-5 min. per pound	5 min.	Turn fish over after ½ of time. Defrost remaining time; rinse in cool water.
Shrimp	50%	3-5 min. per pound	3-5 min.	Rearrange after ⅓ of time and after ⅔ of time. Defrost remaining time; rinse in cool water.

APPETIZERS

With a microwave oven, you can serve a variety of tempting hot appetizers without special warming equipment or last-minute fuss. Do most of the preparation in advance, then pop a bowl of dip or saucy meat tidbits into the oven as the doorbell rings. Pictured here are Chili Con Queso Dip, Mini Reubens, and Mini Tostadas.

MINI REUBENS

1 6-ounce box rye melba toast rounds
¼ pound thinly sliced cooked corned beef
1 8-ounce can sauerkraut, rinsed, drained, and snipped
1 cup finely shredded Swiss cheese
2 teaspoons prepared mustard
Caraway seed

Arrange 8 toast rounds around edge of a dinner plate lined with paper toweling. Place 2 in center. Cut corned beef into 1½-inch squares; place on toast rounds. Top each with about 1 teaspoon sauerkraut. Toss the cheese and mustard together until cheese is evenly coated with mustard. Spoon about 1 teaspoon cheese mixture atop sauerkraut on each round; sprinkle caraway seed lightly atop cheese. Micro-cook, uncovered, on 50% (*MEDIUM*) 1 to 2 minutes or until cheese is melted, rotating once. Repeat with remaining toast rounds. Makes about 48 appetizers.

Keep Your Crackers Crisp

Crackers absorb moisture. To keep them dry, spread canapes just before heating and micro-cook them on a non-coated paper plate or a plate lined with a paper towel or napkin.

PINEAPPLE-HERB CHICKEN APPETIZERS

1 tablespoon instant chicken bouillon granules	1 cup fine dry seasoned bread crumbs
⅓ cup hot water	¼ cup finely chopped celery (optional)
1 8-ounce can crushed pineapple	1 tablespoon dried parsley flakes
1 5-ounce can chicken, drained and chopped	Assorted crackers
1 egg	

Dissolve bouillon in hot water. In a medium mixing bowl combine bouillon, *undrained* pineapple, chicken, egg, bread crumbs, celery, and parsley flakes. Mix until well blended but pineapple is still chunky. Drop by rounded teaspoonfuls onto crackers. Arrange 8 crackers in a circle on a dinner plate lined with 2 layers of paper toweling. Place 1 or 2 crackers in center of circle. Micro-cook, uncovered, on 100% (*HIGH*) 1 to 2 minutes or until hot, rotating a half-turn after 30 seconds. Repeat with remaining appetizers. Makes 50 appetizers.

TUNA AND CHEESE APPETIZERS

1 3¼-ounce can tuna, drained	1 tablespoon snipped parsley
½ cup shredded cheddar cheese (2 ounces)	1 tablespoon finely chopped celery
2 tablespoons mayonnaise *or* salad dressing	½ teaspoon minced dried onion
2 tablespoons fine dry bread crumbs	Wheat wafers

In a small bowl mix together tuna, cheese, mayonnaise or salad dressing, bread crumbs, parsley, celery, and onion with a fork. Drop by teaspoonfuls onto crackers. Arrange in an 8-inch ring on a paper towel-lined dinner plate or pie plate. Place 2 crackers in center of ring. Micro-cook, uncovered, on 50% (*MEDIUM*) 30 seconds to 1½ minutes or until cheese is melted, rotating a quarter-turn after 30 seconds then every 15 seconds. Makes about 30 appetizers.

MINI TOSTADAS

½ of a 16-ounce can refried beans (1 cup)	½ cup shredded cheddar cheese
24 round tortilla chips	24 slices cherry tomatoes (6 to 8 tomatoes)
¼ cup taco sauce	

Spread 1 heaping teaspoon beans on each chip. Top each with ½ teaspoon taco sauce; add 1 teaspoon cheese.

Place 6 to 8 appetizers on a dinner plate lined with paper toweling. Micro-cook, uncovered, on 50% (*MEDIUM*) 1 to 3 minutes or until cheese is melted, rotating a quarter-turn after the first minute, then every 30 seconds. Top each with a tomato slice. Makes 24 appetizers.

GLAZED FRANKFURTERS

1 **16-ounce package frankfurters**	3 **tablespoons brown sugar**
¼ **cup vinegar**	3 **tablespoons honey**
1 **tablespoon cornstarch**	½ **teaspoon ground ginger**
⅓ **cup soy sauce**	½ **teaspoon garlic powder**
¼ **cup water**	⅛ **teaspoon cayenne**
	⅛ **teaspoon ground cloves**

Cut frankfurters diagonally into 1½-inch pieces. Set aside. In a large bowl blend vinegar and cornstarch. Add soy sauce, water, brown sugar, honey, ginger, garlic powder, cayenne, and cloves; mix well. Micro-cook, uncovered, on 100% (*HIGH*) 4 to 6 minutes or until slightly thickened, stirring every 2 minutes. Stir frankfurters into hot sauce. Micro-cook, uncovered, on 50% (*MEDIUM*) 7 to 10 minutes or until frankfurters are thoroughly heated; stir once. Makes 40 appetizers.

HOT SHRIMP CHEESE DIP

1 **cup chopped fresh mushrooms**	1 **4¼-ounce can tiny shrimp, drained**
2 **tablespoons chopped onion**	1 **tablespoon dried parsley flakes**
2 **tablespoons butter *or* margarine**	¼ **teaspoon garlic powder**
1 **10¾-ounce can condensed cream of shrimp soup**	¼ **teaspoon paprika**
	6 **or 7 drops bottled hot pepper sauce**
1 **cup shredded sharp cheddar cheese**	**Unsalted crackers and vegetable dippers**

In a 1½-quart casserole micro-cook mushrooms and onions in butter or margarine, uncovered, on 100% (*HIGH*) 3½ to 4½ minutes, stirring after 2 minutes. Drain. Stir in soup, cheese, shrimp, parsley, garlic powder, paprika, and hot pepper sauce. Micro-cook, uncovered, on 100% (*HIGH*) 4 to 6 minutes or until cheese is melted and mixture is hot, stirring every 2 minutes. Serve hot with unsalted crackers and vegetable dippers. Makes 2 cups.

CHILI CON QUESO DIP

2 **cups shredded American cheese (8 ounces)**	⅛ **teaspoon white pepper**
½ **cup shredded cheddar cheese (2 ounces)**	¼ **cup canned green chilies, drained, seeded, and chopped (about 2 ounces)**
1 **tablespoon all-purpose flour**	¾ **cup light cream**
1 **teaspoon sugar**	**Vegetable dippers**
¼ **teaspoon salt**	

In a 1½-quart casserole mix cheeses and flour. Stir in sugar, salt, and white pepper. Stir in green chilies. Stir in light cream. Micro-cook, uncovered, on 50% (*MEDIUM*) 4 to 6½ minutes or until cheeses are melted and dip is hot, stirring well every 2 minutes. Serve hot with vegetable dippers. Makes 1¾ cups.

Quick Warm-Ups

Serve dips and Glazed Frankfurters in microwave oven-safe dishes. If they need reheating, return them to the oven at the setting used in the recipe. (Remember, less food takes less time.) Appetizers cooked at 50% (MEDIUM) may be reheated on 100% (HIGH) if you stir them more frequently.

SOUPS

Fresh, homemade soups are made easy with the microwave. In this section, you'll find hearty main-dish soups for supper, as well as delicate soups to serve as a first course or light lunch.

HEARTY VEGETABLE SOUP

1 pound boneless beef chuck *or* round steak, cut into ½-inch cubes	3 cups hot water
	3 medium carrots, thinly sliced (about 1½ cups)
2 cups hot water	1 large potato, cut into ½-inch cubes (about 1½ cups)
⅓ cup pearl barley	
1 small onion, sliced	
2 teaspoons salt	1 small onion, sliced
2 teaspoons Worcestershire sauce	1½ cups shredded cabbage
	1 cup frozen baby lima beans
½ teaspoon dried basil, crushed	
⅛ teaspoon pepper	½ teaspoon Kitchen Bouquet
1 bay leaf	

In a 4-quart casserole combine meat, 2 cups hot water, barley, 1 onion, salt, Worcestershire sauce, basil, pepper, and bay leaf. Micro-cook, covered, on 100% (*HIGH*) 5 minutes. Reduce power to 50% (*MEDIUM*). Micro-cook 30 minutes, stirring once during cooking.

Stir in 3 cups hot water, the carrots, potato, 1 onion, and cabbage. Micro-cook, covered, on 50% (*MEDIUM*) 25 minutes, stirring once during cooking. Add beans. Micro-cook, covered, on 50% (*MEDIUM*) 10 to 25 minutes or until meat and vegetables are tender. Let stand, covered, 10 minutes. Stir in Kitchen Bouquet. Remove bay leaf. Makes 6 to 8 servings.

FRENCH ONION SOUP

3 medium onions, thinly sliced and separated into rings (1½ cups)	4 slices French bread, toasted
¼ cup butter *or* margarine	¾ cup shredded Swiss cheese (3 ounces)
2 10½-ounce cans condensed beef broth	¾ cup shredded mozzarella cheese (3 ounces)
2 cups hot water	3 tablespoons grated Parmesan cheese

In a 3-quart casserole combine onions and butter or margarine. Micro-cook, covered, on 100% (*HIGH*) 8 to 11 minutes or until onions are tender, stirring after half the cooking time. Stir in beef broth and hot water. Micro-cook, covered, on 100% (*HIGH*) 4 to 6 minutes or until heated through, stirring once during cooking.

Ladle soup into 4 large individual bowls or casseroles. Top with bread slices. Sprinkle evenly with cheeses. Micro-cook, uncovered, 3 to 5 minutes or until cheeses melt, rearranging bowls once or twice during cooking. Makes 4 servings.

CORN CHOWDER

¼ pound bulk pork sausage	⅛ teaspoon pepper
1 small onion, chopped (¼ cup)	4 cups milk
3 tablespoons all-purpose flour	1 16-ounce can whole potatoes, drained and cut into ½-inch pieces, *or* 1¾ cups cooked cubed potatoes
1 teaspoon snipped chives *or* 1 tablespoon sliced green onion	
½ teaspoon salt	1 16-ounce can cream-style corn

In a 3- to 5-quart casserole combine sausage and onion. Micro-cook, uncovered, on 100% (*HIGH*) 5 minutes or until sausage is cooked, stirring to break up sausage after half the cooking time. (Do not drain.) Stir in flour, chives or green onion, salt, and pepper. Stir in milk. Micro-cook, uncovered, on 100% (*HIGH*) 10 minutes or until bubbly and slightly thickened, stirring three times during cooking.

Stir in potatoes and corn. Micro-cook, uncovered, on 100% (*HIGH*) 5 minutes or until hot, stirring after half the cooking time. Season to taste with additional salt and pepper, if desired. Makes 6 to 8 servings.

How to Cook Potato Cubes

To cook 1¾ cups of ½-inch potato cubes, combine potatoes, ½ cup hot water, and ½ teaspoon salt in a 1-quart casserole. Micro-cook, covered, on 100% (HIGH) 5 to 7 minutes or until tender, stirring once. Drain.

SPLIT PEA SOUP

8 cups hot water	¼ teaspoon dried basil, crushed
1 pound dry green split peas (2¼ cups)	1 bay leaf
2 pounds meaty ham bone	2 medium carrots, thinly sliced (about 1 cup)
½ cup chopped onion	1 large potato, peeled and cut into ½-inch cubes (about 1½ cups)
½ to 1 teaspoon salt	
¼ teaspoon pepper	
¼ teaspoon dried oregano, crushed	

In a 4-quart casserole combine water, split peas, ham bone, onion, salt, pepper, oregano, basil, and bay leaf. Micro-cook, covered, on 100% (*HIGH*) 40 to 50 minutes or until peas are cooked, stirring three times during cooking.

Remove ham bone; cut off and dice ham. Return ham to soup; add carrots and potato. Micro-cook, uncovered, on 100% (*HIGH*) 20 to 25 minutes or until vegetables are tender, stirring three times during cooking . Remove bay leaf. Makes 6 to 8 servings.

No Ham Bone?

Two to three cups diced fully cooked ham may be substituted for the ham bone.

BEAN, BACON, AND VEGETABLE SOUP

1 pound dry navy beans (2½ cups)	¼ teaspoon pepper
7 cups hot water	2 cups hot water
2 teaspoons instant beef bouillon granules	1 medium onion, cut into eighths
1 clove garlic, minced	3 stalks celery, thinly sliced (1½ cups)
1 teaspoon salt	3 medium carrots, thinly sliced (1½ cups)
1 teaspoon dried parsley flakes	8 slices bacon, cut into eighths
½ teaspoon dried marjoram, crushed	

Place beans in a 4- or 5-quart casserole. Stir in 7 cups hot water, the bouillon granules, garlic, salt, parsley flakes, marjoram, and pepper. Micro-cook, covered, on 100% (*HIGH*) 15 to 17 minutes or until water begins to boil. Boil 2 minutes, covered, on 100% (*HIGH*). Let stand 1 hour. (*Or,* combine beans, water, and seasonings; cover and let soak overnight.)

Micro-cook, covered, on 100% (*HIGH*) 45 to 55 minutes or until beans are tender, stirring once or twice. Mash beans slightly for thickened broth. Add 2 cups hot water and the vegetables. Micro-cook, covered, on 100% (*HIGH*) 25 to 35 minutes or until vegetables are tender, stirring once or twice. Let stand, covered, 10 minutes. Meanwhile, in a bowl micro-cook bacon, covered, on 100% (*HIGH*) 6 to 8 minutes or until cooked. Drain off all but 2 tablespoons fat. Stir bacon and reserved drippings into soup. Makes 8 servings.

Microwaving Cream

The cream in this hearty Clam Chowder and the Vichyssoise on the facing page can be microwaved at High power because it is stabilized by flour or mashed potatoes. Without a stabilizer, cream should be microwaved at Medium power or stirred frequently to prevent curdling.

NEW ENGLAND CLAM CHOWDER

4 slices bacon, cut into eighths	¼ cup all-purpose flour
3 potatoes, peeled and cut into ½-inch cubes (3 cups)	1¼ cups milk
	1 teaspoon salt
	⅛ teaspoon pepper
1 small onion, chopped	½ cup light cream
½ cup milk	2 6½-ounce cans minced clams

Micro-cook bacon in a 2-quart casserole, covered, on 100% (*HIGH*) 3½ to 4½ minutes or until crisp. Drain, reserving 2 tablespoons drippings. Add potatoes and onion to bacon. Micro-cook, covered, on 100% (*HIGH*) 7½ to 9 minutes or until potatoes are tender, stirring once during cooking.

Combine ½ cup milk and the flour; add to casserole with 1¼ cups milk, the salt, and pepper. Micro-cook, uncovered, on 100% (*HIGH*) 4½ to 5½ minutes or until thickened and bubbly, stirring every minute. Stir in cream and *undrained* clams. Micro-cook, uncovered, on 100% (*HIGH*) 3 to 4 minutes or until heated through. Makes 4 to 6 servings.

LEMONY CHICKEN BROTH

1 stalk celery, sliced (½ cup)	2 10¾-ounce cans condensed chicken broth
1 small carrot, thinly sliced (⅓ cup)	1⅔ cups water
2 tablespoons butter *or* margarine	1 tablespoon lemon juice
	Dash ginger

In a 2-quart casserole combine celery, carrot, and butter or margarine. Micro-cook, covered, on 100% (*HIGH*) 3½ to 5½ minutes or until vegetables are tender. Stir in broth, water, lemon juice, and ginger. Micro-cook, covered, on 100% (*HIGH*) 6 to 9 minutes or until heated through. Strain. Makes 4 to 6 servings.

SPICY CONSOMMÉ

2 cups sliced fresh mushrooms	¼ teaspoon Worcestershire sauce
1 tablespoon butter *or* margarine	¼ teaspoon chili powder
2 10½-ounce cans condensed beef consommé	¼ teaspoon dried basil, crushed
1¾ cups hot water	¼ teaspoon dried marjoram, crushed
	1 small bay leaf

In a medium bowl combine mushrooms and butter or margarine. Micro-cook, covered, on 100% (*HIGH*) 2 to 3 minutes or until mushrooms are tender. Set aside. In a 2-quart casserole combine consommé, water, Worcestershire sauce, chili powder, basil, marjoram, and bay leaf. Micro-cook, covered, on 100% (*HIGH*) 9 to 10 minutes or until mixture is hot. Remove bay leaf. Add mushrooms. Micro-cook, covered, on 100% (*HIGH*) 3 minutes to blend flavors. Makes 4 to 6 servings.

TOMATO SOUP

1 **28-ounce can whole tomatoes**	⅛ **teaspoon pepper**
2 **tablespoons chopped onion**	3 **tablespoons butter** *or* **margarine**
2 **teaspoons sugar**	3 **tablespoons all-purpose flour**
1 **teaspoon salt**	1½ **cups milk**
¼ **teaspoon dried basil, crushed**	

In a 2-quart casserole combine tomatoes, onion, sugar, salt, basil, and pepper. Micro-cook, uncovered, on 100% (*HIGH*) 15 minutes, stirring once or twice and breaking up tomatoes. Strain, reserving juice. Sieve tomatoes and set aside; discard seeds. Return juice to casserole.

In a small dish micro-cook butter or margarine, uncovered, on 100% (*HIGH*) 30 to 60 seconds or until melted. Stir in flour; stir into tomato juice until smooth. Stir in milk. Micro-cook, uncovered, on 100% (*HIGH*) 5 to 7½ minutes or until thickened, stirring after 2 minutes, then every minute. Stir sieved tomatoes into milk mixture. Micro-cook, uncovered, on 100% (*HIGH*) 1 to 2 minutes to reheat, if necessary. Makes 4 to 6 servings.

QUICK VICHYSSOISE

2 **cups mashed potatoes**	1 **teaspoon dried parsley flakes**
1 **cup hot water**	¼ **teaspoon onion powder**
1 **cup whipping cream**	⅛ **teaspoon white pepper**
1½ **teaspoons Worcestershire sauce**	**Dash garlic powder**
1 **teaspoon instant chicken bouillon granules**	**Dash ground nutmeg**
	Snipped chives

In a 1½- or 2-quart casserole blend potatoes, water, whipping cream, Worcestershire sauce, bouillon granules, parsley flakes, onion powder, white pepper, garlic powder, and nutmeg. Micro-cook, uncovered, on 100% (*HIGH*) 4 to 7 minutes or until bubbly, stirring once or twice during cooking. Serve warm or chilled. Garnish with chives. Makes 4 to 6 servings.

EGG DROP SOUP

3½ **cups hot water**	½ **teaspoon soy sauce**
¼ **cup sliced green onion**	**Dash garlic powder**
5 **teaspoons instant chicken bouillon granules**	3 **beaten eggs**

In a 1½- or 2-quart casserole combine water, onion, bouillon granules, soy sauce, and garlic powder. Micro-cook, covered, on 100% (*HIGH*) 7 to 9 minutes or until mixture boils. Using a circular motion slowly pour eggs into soup in a thin stream. Micro-cook, uncovered, on 100% (*HIGH*) 1 minute to finish cooking eggs, stirring once during cooking. Makes 4 to 6 servings.

How to Freeze Soups for Microwave Reheating

Line a microwave oven-proof soup bowl with a double thickness of foil or clear plastic wrap, or a heavy-duty plastic bag. Fill with 1 serving of soup. Freeze until solid. Remove from bowl, seal, label, and store in the freezer.

To reheat, unwrap and return soup to bowl. Do not freeze soups containing flour or cornstarch because these ingredients break down and become grainy.

MEATS

Make the most of your microwave oven by using it to prepare a variety of meats, from a Sunday roast to a ground beef casserole. Here you'll find meats and main dishes for any occasion.

BEEF STEW

1	cup frozen peas	1	teaspoon sugar
1	1½-pound boneless beef chuck roast, cut into ¾-inch cubes	1	teaspoon dried parsley flakes
⅓	cup all-purpose flour	⅛	teaspoon pepper
1½	cups hot water	1	8-ounce can tomato sauce
1	large onion, sliced	6	medium carrots, thinly sliced
1	bay leaf		
1	tablespoon instant beef bouillon granules	4	medium potatoes, peeled and cut into eighths
1½	teaspoons salt	2	stalks celery, sliced

Measure peas and set aside. In a 3-quart casserole toss meat with flour. Add water, onion, bay leaf, bouillon granules, salt, sugar, parsley flakes, and pepper. Micro-cook, covered, on 100% (*HIGH*) 5 minutes; stir. Reduce power to 50% (*MEDIUM*). Micro-cook 20 minutes, stirring once.

Stir in tomato sauce, carrots, potatoes, and celery. Micro-cook, covered, on 50% (*MEDIUM*) 40 to 60 minutes or until meat and vegetables are tender, stirring once. Add peas; micro-cook on 50% (*MEDIUM*) 1 to 2 minutes or until heated through. Let stand, covered, 10 minutes. Makes 4 to 6 servings.

BROWN STEW

- 6 slices bacon, cut crosswise into eighths
- 2 to 2½ pounds boneless beef chuck roast, cut into ¾-inch cubes
- ⅓ cup all-purpose flour
- 1 tablespoon soy sauce
- 1½ teaspoons seasoned salt
- ¼ teaspoon dried basil, crushed
- ⅛ teaspoon garlic powder
- 1½ cups hot water
- ½ cup dry red wine
- 2 medium onions, cut into eight wedges
- 2 cups sliced fresh mushrooms

In a 3-quart casserole micro-cook bacon, covered, on 100% (*HIGH*) 6 minutes. Drain off fat, reserving 2 tablespoons in casserole. Add beef cubes to casserole. Toss with flour, soy sauce, salt, basil, and garlic powder. Stir in water, wine, and onions. Micro-cook, covered, on 100% (*HIGH*) 5 minutes. Reduce power to 50% (*MEDIUM*). Micro-cook, uncovered, 30 minutes, stirring once. Add mushrooms. Micro-cook, uncovered, on 50% (*MEDIUM*) 35 to 45 minutes or until beef is tender, stirring once. Cover and let stand 10 minutes. Serves 8.

PEPPER STEAK

- 1 tablespoon cornstarch
- ½ teaspoon sugar
- ½ teaspoon salt
- ¼ teaspoon ground ginger
- 1 clove garlic, minced
- ½ cup cold water
- 2 tablespoons soy sauce
- 1 tablespoon cooking oil
- 1 to 1½ pounds beef sirloin steak, thinly sliced into bite-size strips
- 1 tablespoon cooking oil
- 2 stalks celery, thinly sliced (1 cup)
- 1 medium onion, thinly sliced (1 cup)
- 1 medium green pepper, cut into thin strips
- 1 2-ounce jar diced pimiento, drained
- Hot cooked rice *or* chow mein noodles

Mix cornstarch, sugar, salt, ginger, and garlic; stir in water, soy sauce, and 1 tablespoon cooking oil. Add meat and toss. Let stand 10 minutes to marinate.

Preheat a 10-inch microwave browning dish on 100% (*HIGH*) 5 minutes. Add 1 tablespoon oil; swirl to coat dish. Add meat mixture. Micro-cook, uncovered, on 100% (*HIGH*) 2 minutes or until meat loses most of its pink color, stirring 3 times.

Add celery, onion, green pepper, and pimiento. Micro-cook, uncovered, on 100% (*HIGH*) 6 to 9 minutes or until vegetables are crisp-tender, stirring after half the cooking time. Serve on rice or chow mein noodles. Pass additional soy sauce, if desired. Makes 4 servings.

BEEF STROGANOFF

1½ pounds boneless beef sirloin steak
¼ cup all-purpose flour
8 ounces fresh mushrooms, sliced
1 medium onion, thinly sliced
⅔ cup beef broth
2 tablespoons catsup
1 tablespoon butter *or* margarine
1 teaspoon dry mustard
½ teaspoon salt
¼ teaspoon pepper
1 cup dairy sour cream
2 tablespoons all-purpose flour
2 tablespoons dry white wine
Hot cooked rice *or* noodles

Partially freeze steak; thinly slice into bite-size strips. In a 3-quart casserole toss beef with ¼ cup flour. Stir in mushrooms, onion, beef broth, catsup, butter or margarine, mustard, salt, and pepper. Micro-cook, covered, on 100% (*HIGH*) 5 minutes; stir. Reduce power to 50% (*MEDIUM*). Micro-cook, covered, 18 to 33 minutes or until meat is tender, stirring after half the cooking time. Meanwhile, blend together sour cream, 2 tablespoons flour, and dry white wine. Gradually add about 1 cup of the hot mixture to sour cream; stir into mixture in casserole. Micro-cook, uncovered, on 100% (*HIGH*) 6 minutes or till thickened and bubbly, stirring every 2 minutes. Serve over rice or noodles. Makes 4 to 6 servings.

MARINATED POT ROAST

1 cup catsup
⅓ cup packed brown sugar
1 tablespoon Worcestershire sauce
1 tablespoon vinegar
1 teaspoon dry mustard
¼ teaspoon chili powder
⅛ teaspoon pepper
Dash allspice
1 2½- to 3½-pound beef chuck blade pot roast

Combine catsup, brown sugar, Worcestershire sauce, vinegar, mustard, chili powder, pepper, and allspice. Pierce roast with a fork on all sides. Place roast in an oven cooking bag; set in a shallow baking dish. Add catsup mixture to bag; tie loosely with a narrow strip cut from open end of bag. Refrigerate 12 hours or overnight. Occasionally press bag against roast to distribute marinade.

Micro-cook, in bag, on 100% (*HIGH*) 5 minutes. Reduce power to 50% (*MEDIUM*). Micro-cook 20 to 30 minutes per pound or until meat is tender, rotating bag a half-turn every 30 minutes. After half of the cooking time, turn entire bag over. Let stand 10 minutes. Skim fat from sauce; baste meat with sauce. Makes 4 to 6 servings.

Tips for Micro-waved Pot Roasts

Select a flat roast, such as blade or arm, for even cooking. When using an oven cooking bag, tie the bag loosely to allow excess steam to escape. Do not use metal twist ties; they may cause the cooking bag to melt.

How to Use Large Carrots

If carrots are more than ½ inch thick, cut in half lengthwise.

POT ROAST WITH VEGETABLES Pictured on the cover

½ cup water
1 tablespoon Worcester-shire sauce
1 teaspoon salt
¼ teaspoon pepper
¼ teaspoon dried thyme, crushed
⅛ teaspoon garlic powder
1 tablespoon all-purpose flour

1 3-pound beef chuck pot roast
2 medium onions, cut into eighths
4 medium carrots, cut into 1-inch pieces
3 to 3½ cups cubed potatoes (2 to 3 medium potatoes)
1 10-ounce package frozen cut green beans

Combine water, Worcestershire sauce, salt, pepper, thyme, and garlic powder. Sprinkle flour inside an oven cooking bag. Place meat in bag; set in a 12×7½×2-inch baking dish or 5-quart casserole. Add water mixture. Seal cooking bag by tying loosely with a narrow strip cut from open end of bag. Pierce bag in several places.

Micro-cook on 100% (*HIGH*) 5 minutes. Reduce power to 50% (*MEDIUM*). Micro-cook 35 minutes. Turn roast over; add vegetables. Seal as before. Micro-cook on 50% (*MEDIUM*) 35 to 50 minutes or until meat and vegetables are tender. Let stand 10 minutes. Makes 6 servings.

FREEZER-TO-TABLE ROAST

1 3- to 3½-pound frozen beef chuck pot roast
1 1¼-ounce envelope *regular* onion soup mix

1 10¾-ounce can condensed cream of mushroom soup
1 4-ounce can mushroom stems and pieces

Place unwrapped* frozen roast in a 12×7½×2-inch baking dish. Cover with vented plastic wrap. Micro-cook on 100% (*HIGH*) 3 minutes. Reduce power to 50% (*MEDIUM*). Micro-cook, covered, 10 to 15 minutes per pound. Rotate dish after 25 minutes.

Drain liquid from baking dish. Sprinkle *half* of the dry soup mix over top of roast; turn over. Sprinkle with remaining soup mix. Combine mushroom soup and *undrained* mushrooms; spread over roast. Micro-cook, covered, on 50% (*MEDIUM*) 10 to 15 minutes more per pound or till tender; stir and spoon sauce over roast after half the cooking time. Let stand, covered, 10 minutes. Makes 6 to 8 servings.

*If necessary, remove remaining wrapping from roast after meat is partly cooked.

ROLLED STUFFED MEAT LOAF

1½ **pounds ground beef**
¼ **cup fine dry bread crumbs**
2 **eggs**
1 **teaspoon salt**
1 **teaspoon onion powder**
½ **teaspoon dry mustard**
1 **small carrot, shredded (⅓ cup)**

⅓ **cup chopped celery**
2 **tablespoons butter *or* margarine**
1½ **cups herb-seasoned stuffing croutons, crushed**
1 **4-ounce can mushroom stems and pieces, drained**
⅓ **cup hot water**

Combine beef, bread crumbs, eggs, salt, onion powder, and dry mustard. On waxed paper, pat into a 12×8-inch rectangle.

In a small bowl or casserole micro-cook carrot, celery, and butter or margarine, uncovered, on 100% (*HIGH*) 2 to 3 minutes or until tender. Stir in crushed croutons, mushrooms, and water. Spread carrot mixture over meat, leaving a 1-inch border on all sides. Starting with short side, roll meat loaf jelly roll style; use waxed paper to lift. Press edges together to seal. Place in an 8×4×2-inch loaf dish, seam side down.

Micro-cook, uncovered, on 100% (*HIGH*) 5 minutes. Reduce power to 50% (*MEDIUM*). Micro-cook 10 to 25 minutes or until meat is firm and loses its pink color, and internal temperature is 150°, rotating dish a half-turn after half the cooking time or as needed. Let stand 5 minutes. Serves 4 to 6.

SAUCED MEAT LOAF

⅓ **cup finely crushed saltine crackers**
¼ **cup milk**
4 **slices bacon**
1½ **pounds ground beef**
2 **beaten eggs**
1 **small onion, chopped (about ⅓ cup)**

1 **teaspoon salt**
¼ **teaspoon pepper**
¼ **cup chili sauce**
2 **tablespoons brown sugar**
1 **teaspoon prepared mustard**

In a small bowl combine crushed crackers and milk; set aside. In a 2-quart casserole micro-cook bacon on 100% (*HIGH*) 3 to 4 minutes or until crisp; remove from casserole. Crumble bacon and return to drippings in casserole. Add ground beef, eggs, onion, salt, pepper, and cracker mixture to casserole; mix thoroughly. Spoon into an 8×4×2-inch loaf dish. Micro-cook, uncovered, on 100% (*HIGH*) 10 to 15 minutes or until internal temperature is 130°, rotating dish every 4 or 5 minutes. Drain off excess fat.

In a small mixing bowl combine chili sauce, brown sugar, and mustard. Pour *half* of chili sauce mixture over meat loaf. Micro-cook, uncovered, on 50% (*MEDIUM*) 2 minutes. Pour remaining sauce mixture over meat loaf. Micro-cook, uncovered, on 50% (*MEDIUM*) 1½ to 4 minutes or until internal temperature is 145°. Let stand 5 minutes. Makes 6 servings.

Testing Doneness with a Conventional Meat Thermometer

If you don't have a micro-wave thermometer or probe, you can use a con-ventional thermometer outside the oven. Insert it so the bulb is in the center of the meat loaf, and let stand about 1 minute. If the internal temperature is not high enough, remove the thermometer and micro-cook the meat loaf a little longer. Do not use a conventional thermometer inside the microwave oven.

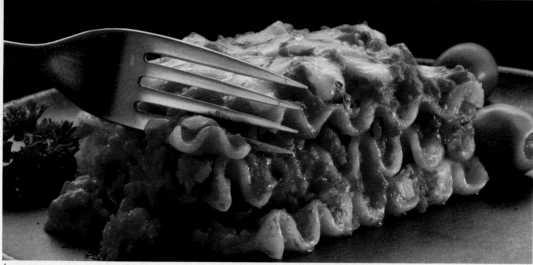

Lasagne

LASAGNE

5 **cups hot water**	1 **teaspoon dried basil, crushed**
1 **tablespoon cooking oil**	1 **teaspoon dried oregano, crushed**
9 **uncooked lasagne noodles**	1 **teaspoon brown sugar**
1 **pound ground beef**	¼ **teaspoon pepper**
¼ **pound bulk pork sausage**	½ **of a 15-ounce carton (1 cup) ricotta cheese**
1 **medium onion, thinly sliced**	2 **eggs**
½ **medium green pepper, chopped (¼ cup)**	½ **cup grated Parmesan cheese**
1 **clove garlic, minced**	1 **tablespoon dried parsley flakes**
1 **16-ounce can tomatoes, cut up**	½ **teaspoon dried basil**
1 **12-ounce can tomato paste**	2 **cups shredded mozzarella cheese**

Combine water, oil, and ½ teaspoon *salt* in a 12×7½×2-inch baking dish. Cover tightly with vented clear plastic wrap. Micro-cook on 100% (*HIGH*) 8 to 10 minutes or until water boils. Add noodles. Micro-cook, covered, on 100% (*HIGH*) 5½ to 8 minutes or until noodles are tender but still firm, rotating dish a half-turn after half the cooking time. Rinse noodles well under cool water. Spread on paper toweling to drain.

Combine ground beef, pork sausage, onion, green pepper, and garlic in a 3-quart casserole. Micro-cook, uncovered, on 100% (*HIGH*) 6 minutes or until meat loses its pink color, stirring to break up meat after half the cooking time. Drain. Stir in tomatoes, tomato paste, 1 teaspoon basil, the oregano, brown sugar, pepper, and 1½ teaspoons *salt*. Micro-cook, covered, on 100% (*HIGH*) 5 minutes. Stir. Reduce power to 50% (*MEDIUM*). Micro-cook, uncovered, 5 minutes or until heated through, stirring once.

In a medium bowl mix ricotta, eggs, Parmesan, parsley flakes, and ½ teaspoon basil. In a 12×7½×2-inch baking dish, layer ⅓ each of the noodles, ricotta mixture, meat sauce, and mozzarella. Repeat twice, reserving the last ⅓ mozzarella. Micro-cook, uncovered, on 50% (*MEDIUM*) 20 to 28 minutes or until bubbly, sprinkling reserved mozzarella on top and rotating dish a half-turn after 15 minutes. Let stand 10 to 15 minutes. Makes 8 servings.

CHILI

1 pound ground beef
1 medium onion, chopped
½ cup chopped celery
1 16-ounce can stewed tomatoes
1 15-ounce can red kidney beans, drained
1 10¾-ounce can condensed tomato soup
1 to 2 teaspoons chili powder
1 teaspoon brown sugar
½ teaspoon salt
⅛ teaspoon pepper
⅛ teaspoon dried oregano, crushed
Dash cayenne

Crumble ground beef into a 2½-quart casserole. Add onion and celery. Micro-cook, uncovered, on 100% (HIGH) 4 to 6 minutes or until meat is almost cooked, stirring after half the cooking time to break up meat. Drain.

Add undrained tomatoes, kidney beans, tomato soup, chili powder, brown sugar, salt, pepper, oregano, and cayenne. Micro-cook, covered, on 100% (HIGH) 5 minutes. Stir. Reduce power to 50% (MEDIUM). Micro-cook, uncovered, 15 to 25 minutes or until of desired consistency, stirring at least once. Makes about 2 quarts.

HAMBURGERS

1 pound ground beef

Shape ground beef into 4 patties, ¾ inch thick. On 100% (HIGH) preheat microwave browning dish 5 minutes or browning grill 6½ minutes. Place patties in browning dish or grill. Micro-cook, uncovered, on 100% (HIGH) 2 minutes. Turn over patties. Micro-cook, uncovered, on 100% (HIGH) 1½ to 2¾ minutes. Season to taste. Makes 4 servings.

SWEDISH MEATBALLS

¼ cup milk
1 egg
½ cup fine dry bread crumbs
1 teaspoon salt
⅛ teaspoon pepper
⅛ teaspoon ground allspice
⅛ teaspoon ground nutmeg
1 pound ground beef
½ pound ground pork
½ cup chopped onion
2 tablespoons all-purpose flour
⅛ to ¼ teaspoon dried dillweed
⅛ teaspoon salt
1 cup whipping cream

In a large bowl combine milk and egg; stir in bread crumbs, 1 teaspoon salt, the pepper, allspice, and nutmeg. Mix in beef, pork, and onion. Shape into 1-inch meatballs; arrange in a 12×7½×2-inch baking dish. Micro-cook, uncovered, on 100% (HIGH) 8 to 13 minutes or until firm and no longer pink, rearranging once or twice during cooking so least-cooked meatballs are brought to edges of dish.

Push meatballs to one end of dish. Drain off fat. In the baking dish stir together flour, dillweed, and salt; gradually stir in cream. Micro-cook, uncovered, on 50% (MEDIUM) 4 to 8 minutes or until slightly thickened, stirring well every 2 minutes. Makes 4 to 6 servings.

Use Some and Freeze Some

If you're cooking chili for one or two people, serve what you need and freeze the rest. For quick defrosting and heating, divide into single servings and package in shallow freezer boxes or heat-sealable bags.

Microwaving Extracts More Fat

It's important to drain the meat when making spaghetti sauce or chow mein, because microwaving extracts more fat than conventional cooking.

BEEF AND PORK CHOW MEIN

½ **pound ground beef**	¼ **teaspoon ground ginger**
½ **pound ground pork**	1 **16-ounce can chow mein**
1 **medium onion, sliced**	**vegetables, drained**
and separated into rings	1 **8-ounce can sliced water**
1 **medium green pepper,**	**chestnuts, drained**
cut into thin strips	2 **tablespoons dry sherry**
1 **cup sliced celery**	**(optional)**
1½ **cups water**	**Hot cooked rice or**
¼ **cup soy sauce**	**warmed chow mein**
¼ **cup cornstarch**	**noodles**
1 **teaspoon instant beef**	
bouillon granules	

Crumble ground meats into a 2-quart casserole. Micro-cook, uncovered, on 100% (*HIGH*) 4 to 5 minutes or till meat loses its pink color, stirring once to break up meat. Drain meat well; set aside. In same casserole combine onion, green pepper, and celery. Micro-cook, covered, on 100% (*HIGH*) 3 to 4 minutes or till crisp-tender. Set aside.

In a 4-cup measure combine water, soy sauce, cornstarch, bouillon granules, and ginger until smooth. Micro-cook, uncovered, on 100% (*HIGH*) 5 to 6 minutes or till thickened, stirring after 2 minutes, then every minute. To vegetables in casserole, add soy sauce mixture, meat, chow mein vegetables, water chestnuts, and sherry. Micro-cook, covered, on 100% (*HIGH*) 3 to 4 minutes or till heated through, stirring once. Serve over rice or chow mein noodles. Pass additional soy sauce, if desired. Makes 4 servings.

SPAGHETTI

1 **pound ground beef**	⅓ **cup chopped pimiento-**
½ **cup chopped onion**	**stuffed olives**
1 **small carrot, finely**	1 **bay leaf**
chopped (⅓ cup)	2 **teaspoons sugar**
1 **clove garlic, minced**	1 **teaspoon salt**
1 **16-ounce can whole**	1 **teaspoon dried basil,**
tomatoes, cut up	**crushed**
1 **6-ounce can tomato paste**	½ **teaspoon dried oregano,**
½ **cup dry red wine or**	**crushed**
tomato sauce	¼ **teaspoon pepper**
	Hot cooked spaghetti

Crumble ground beef into a 2-quart casserole. Add onion, carrot, and garlic. Micro-cook, covered, on 100% (*HIGH*) 5 minutes. Stir to break up meat; drain.

Stir in *undrained* tomatoes, tomato paste, wine or tomato sauce, olives, bay leaf, sugar, salt, basil, oregano, and pepper. Micro-cook, covered, on 50% (*MEDIUM*) 20 minutes; uncover and cook 10 minutes longer or until of desired thickness, stirring at least once during cooking. Remove bay leaf. Serve with hot cooked spaghetti. Makes 6 servings.

STUFFED ZUCCHINI

2 medium zucchini (about 1⅓ pounds)
¼ teaspoon salt
½ pound ground beef
2 tablespoons chopped green pepper
1 tablespoon minced dried onion
1 8-ounce can whole kernel corn, drained
¼ cup fine dry bread crumbs
½ teaspoon seasoned salt
1 cup shredded cheddar cheese (4 ounces)

Halve zucchini lengthwise. Micro-cook zucchini on 100% (*HIGH*) 5 to 7 minutes. Scoop out, leaving a ¼-inch shell. Coarsely chop enough zucchini pulp to make 1 cup; discard remainder. Sprinkle zucchini shells with ¼ teaspoon salt. Set aside, cut side down, to drain.

In a 1½-quart casserole combine ground beef, green pepper, onion, and the 1 cup zucchini pulp. Micro-cook, uncovered, on 100% (*HIGH*) 3 to 4 minutes or until meat loses its pink color. Break up meat; drain. Stir in corn, bread crumbs, and seasoned salt. Mound ¼ of the meat mixture in each zucchini shell. Arrange in an 8×8×2-inch or 12×7½×2-inch baking dish. Cover with vented clear plastic wrap. Micro-cook on 100% (*HIGH*) 3 to 6 minutes or until zucchini shells are almost tender, rotating after 3 minutes. Sprinkle cheese over stuffing. Micro-cook, uncovered, on 100% (*HIGH*) 1 to 3 minutes or until cheese melts. Serves 2.

Micro-Cook Zucchini First

In this recipe, the zucchini are partially cooked so they will finish cooking in the short time it takes to heat the cooked filling. Salting the zucchini extracts excess moisture, so they do not become watery.

SALISBURY STEAK

1 pound ground beef
¼ cup finely crushed saltine crackers
1 beaten egg
1 tablespoon Worcestershire sauce
½ teaspoon salt
1 teaspoon Kitchen Bouquet (optional)
1 teaspoon water
1 ¾-ounce envelope brown gravy mix
1 teaspoon minced dried onion
1 cup water
English muffins or bread, toasted

Combine ground beef, crushed crackers, egg, Worcestershire sauce, and salt. Shape into four ½-inch-thick patties; place in an 8×8×2-inch baking dish. If desired, brush with a mixture of Kitchen Bouquet and 1 teaspoon water. Cover with waxed paper. Micro-cook on 100% (*HIGH*) 4 minutes, rotating dish after half the time.

Turn patties over; brush again with Kitchen Bouquet mixture, if desired. Micro-cook, covered, on 100% (*HIGH*) 2 to 3 minutes. Remove patties to a serving platter; cover to keep warm.

Add gravy mix and minced dried onion to drippings in dish. Stir in 1 cup water. Micro-cook, uncovered, on 100% (*HIGH*) 3 to 4 minutes or until thickened, stirring every minute. Serve on toasted English muffins or bread. Serves 4.

Note: For softer onion in the gravy, soak onion in the 1 cup water while micro-cooking patties.

HAWAIIAN PORK ROAST

1 **3½- to 4½-pound pork loin center rib roast**	¼ **teaspoon garlic powder**
Whole cloves	⅛ **teaspoon ground ginger**
1½ **cups packed brown sugar**	⅔ **cup unsweetened pineapple juice**
2 **tablespoons water**	3 **tablespoons honey**
1 **tablespoon dry white wine *or* dry sherry**	2 **tablespoons soy sauce**
1 **tablespoon prepared mustard**	2 **tablespoons red wine vinegar**
1 **tablespoon cornstarch**	**Canned pineapple slices (optional)**

Score fat side of roast in diamonds (cut only ¼ inch deep). Place whole cloves at intersections of score lines. In a shallow baking dish with a nonmetal rack, place roast fat side down. Micro-cook, uncovered, on 100% (*HIGH*) 5 minutes. Reduce power to 50% (*MEDIUM*); micro-cook 25 minutes. If desired, insert microwave thermometer or probe in meatiest portion, not touching fat or bone. Turn roast fat side up. Combine brown sugar, water, wine, and mustard; spread over roast. Micro-cook on 50% (*MEDIUM*) 20 to 35 minutes longer or until internal temperature reaches 170°, basting 2 or 3 times. Remove from oven; cover with tent of foil and let stand for 10 minutes.

Meanwhile, in a 2-cup measure combine cornstarch, garlic powder, and ginger. Stir in pineapple juice, honey, soy sauce, and vinegar. Micro-cook, uncovered, on 100% (*HIGH*) for 2 to 4 minutes or until thickened and bubbly, stirring every minute. Spoon over roast. Garnish roast with pineapple rings, if desired. Makes 6 servings.

ORIENTAL PORK AND BROCCOLI

1 **tablespoon soy sauce**	⅓ **cup water**
1 **tablespoon cold water**	¼ **cup dry sherry**
1 **tablespoon cornstarch**	2 **tablespoons soy sauce**
1 **tablespoon cooking oil**	1 **tablespoon cooking oil**
1 **pound boneless pork, thinly sliced into bite-size strips**	1 **tablespoon cornstarch**
	½ **pound broccoli, thinly sliced**

In a medium bowl combine 1 tablespoon soy sauce, 1 tablespoon water, and 1 tablespoon cornstarch. Add pork; stir until well coated. Heat a 10-inch microwave browning dish on 100% (*HIGH*) 5 minutes. Add 1 tablespoon oil; add pork. Micro-cook on 100% (*HIGH*) 2 to 4 minutes or until tender, stirring every minute. Remove pork from browning dish.

In a 1-cup measure combine ⅓ cup water, ¼ cup sherry, 2 tablespoons soy sauce, 1 tablespoon oil, and 1 tablespoon cornstarch. Pour into browning dish; add broccoli and toss well. Micro-cook on 100% (*HIGH*) 2 to 6 minutes or until broccoli is crisp-tender, stirring after half the time. Stir in pork. Micro-cook on 100% (*HIGH*) 1 to 3 minutes or until heated through. Makes 4 servings.

Hawaiian Pork Roast

SPARERIBS CANTONESE

3 pounds pork spareribs, cut into serving-size pieces
½ cup orange marmalade
¼ cup soy sauce
¼ teaspoon garlic powder
¼ teaspoon ground ginger
Dash pepper
Orange slices (optional)

Arrange ribs around sides and over bottom of a 12×7½×2-inch baking dish, overlapping slightly as needed. Cover with waxed paper. Micro-cook on 100% (*HIGH*) 10 minutes. Drain well. Rearrange and turn ribs over, so least-cooked pieces are exposed and more-cooked parts are overlapped.

In a small mixing bowl combine marmalade, soy sauce, garlic powder, ginger, and pepper. Spoon sauce over ribs. Micro-cook, covered, on 100% (*HIGH*) 20 minutes or until done, basting and rearranging ribs every 5 minutes. Garnish with orange slices, if desired. Makes 4 servings.

HEARTY MEXICAN STEW

1 **pound lean boneless pork, cut into 1-inch cubes**	1 **8-ounce can whole kernel corn, drained**
1 **small onion, chopped**	1 **teaspoon sugar**
½ **pound zucchini**	½ **teaspoon salt**
1 **16-ounce can tomatoes, cut up**	¼ **teaspoon ground cumin**
	¼ **teaspoon chili powder**
	¼ **teaspoon garlic powder**
	¼ **teaspoon pepper**

In a 2-quart casserole combine pork and onion. Micro-cook, covered, on 100% (*HIGH*) 5 to 7 minutes; stir. Reduce power to 50% (*MEDIUM*); micro-cook 5 to 7 minutes or until meat loses its pink color, stirring once after 4 minutes.

Slice zucchini; halve large slices. Stir zucchini, *undrained* tomatoes, corn, sugar, salt, cumin, chili powder, garlic powder, and pepper into pork mixture. Micro-cook, covered, on 50% (*MEDIUM*) 25 to 35 minutes or until meat and vegetables are tender, stirring every 10 minutes. Let stand, covered, 10 minutes. Makes 4 servings.

PORK CHOPS AND SAUERKRAUT

2 **medium potatoes, peeled and cut into ½-inch cubes (2 cups)**	½ **teaspoon dried thyme, crushed**
1 **27-ounce can sauerkraut**	⅛ **teaspoon pepper**
1 **medium apple, cored and cut into 1-inch cubes**	4 **pork loin chops, ½ inch thick (about 1¾ pounds)**
2 **tablespoons butter *or* margarine**	1½ **teaspoons Kitchen Bouquet**
1 **tablespoon brown sugar**	1 **teaspoon salt**
1 **teaspoon caraway seed**	½ **teaspoon dried thyme, crushed**
½ **teaspoon salt**	1 **medium onion, thinly sliced and separated into rings**

In a 12×7½×2-inch baking dish micro-cook potatoes, covered with clear plastic wrap, on 100% (*HIGH*) 8 to 12 minutes or till tender. Stir in *undrained* sauerkraut and apple. In a small dish micro-cook butter or margarine, uncovered, on 100% (*HIGH*) 30 to 60 seconds or till melted. Stir in brown sugar, caraway seed, ½ teaspoon salt, ½ teaspoon thyme, and pepper. Add to sauerkraut mixture; toss to blend. Place chops atop mixture. In a small bowl combine Kitchen Bouquet, 1 teaspoon salt, and ½ teaspoon thyme. Brush *half* of the mixture over chops. Cover with vented clear plastic wrap. Micro-cook on 50% (*MEDIUM*) 10 minutes, giving dish a half-turn once. Turn chops over; brush with remaining Kitchen Bouquet mixture. Top with onion slices. Micro-cook, covered, on 50% (*MEDIUM*) 14 to 20 minutes or till chops are no longer pink near bone, giving dish a half-turn once. Let stand, covered, 5 minutes before serving. Makes 4 servings.

Microwaving Pork Chops

Pork chops dry out and overcook easily. They should be covered and micro-cooked on 50% (MEDIUM) with ingredients that will provide moisture. In this recipe, the potatoes are micro-cooked on 100% (HIGH) first, since they would not become tender in the time needed to cook pork on 50% (MEDIUM).

HAM AND CHEESE SPAGHETTI BAKE
Pictured on the cover

6 **green onions, sliced**	½ **teaspoon celery salt**
1 **4-ounce can sliced mushrooms, drained**	¼ **teaspoon pepper**
2 **tablespoons butter *or* margarine**	8 **ounces spaghetti, cooked and drained**
1 **cup cream-style cottage cheese**	3 **cups cubed fully cooked ham**
1 **cup dairy sour cream**	1 **cup shredded cheddar cheese (4 ounces)**

In a 12×7½×2-inch baking dish combine onions, mushrooms, and butter or margarine; cover with clear plastic wrap. Micro-cook on 100% (*HIGH*) 3½ minutes, stirring once.

Stir in cottage cheese, sour cream, celery salt, and pepper. Add spaghetti and ham; mix well. Micro-cook, covered, on 100% (*HIGH*) 12 to 14 minutes, giving dish a quarter-turn twice. Sprinkle cheese over top. Cover; let stand 5 minutes to melt cheese. Makes 6 to 8 servings.

HAM AND POTATOES AU GRATIN

4 **medium potatoes, peeled and sliced ¼ inch thick**	½ **teaspoon dried basil, crushed**
1 **medium onion, thinly sliced**	¼ **teaspoon dry mustard**
¼ **cup hot water**	½ **cup whipping cream *or* light cream**
½ **teaspoon salt**	1 **cup diced fully cooked ham**
3 **tablespoons butter *or* margarine**	1 **cup shredded cheddar cheese (4 ounces)**
3 **tablespoons all-purpose flour**	

In an 8×8×2-inch baking dish, arrange potatoes and onion. Add hot water and salt; cover with vented clear plastic wrap. Micro-cook on 100% (*HIGH*) 7 to 9 minutes or until potatoes are cooked but firm, rotating dish a quarter-turn every 3 minutes.

In a 2-cup measure or small bowl, micro-cook butter or margarine on 100% (*HIGH*) 30 to 45 seconds or until melted. Stir in flour, basil, and mustard until smooth. Gradually blend in cream.

Pour cream mixture over vegetables; sprinkle with ham and cheese. Stir gently. Micro-cook, covered, on 50% (*MEDIUM*) 5 to 7 minutes or until mixture is hot and cheese is melted, rotating dish a quarter-turn every 2 minutes. Let stand, covered, 10 minutes. Makes 4 to 6 servings.

Rotate Foods That Cannot Be Stirred

In these recipes, stirring would break up the potatoes and spaghetti, so the dishes are rotated during cooking to help distribute heat evenly.

German Potato Salad
and Bologna

SOUTHERN BAKED HAM

1 **5-pound fully cooked boneless rolled ham**	3 **tablespoons brown sugar**
¼ **cup packed brown sugar Whole cloves**	2 **tablespoons cornstarch**
¼ **cup packed brown sugar**	4 **teaspoons prepared mustard**
1 **8-ounce can pineapple slices**	1 **tablespoon light corn syrup**
4 **maraschino cherries**	⅛ **teaspoon ground ginger**

Score ham fat in diamonds, cutting only ¼ inch deep. Place ham, fat side down, in a shallow baking dish. Pat top with ¼ cup brown sugar. Cover cut surface of ham with clear plastic wrap. Insert microwave thermometer or probe so tip is in center of meat. Shield upper cut edge with foil, if needed, to prevent over-cooking. Micro-cook on 50% (*MEDIUM*) 30 minutes.

Turn ham over. Insert cloves at each intersection in diamond pattern. Pat with ¼ cup brown sugar. Drain pineapple, reserving the juice. Arrange pineapple slices on top of ham and place a cherry in the center of each slice. Secure with wooden picks. Insert thermometer, if used. Place shielding, if used, on top edge of ham. Micro-cook on 50% (*MEDIUM*) 20 to 45 minutes or until internal temperature reaches 120°.

In a 1-quart casserole or medium bowl combine 3 tablespoons brown sugar, the cornstarch, and mustard. Blend in reserved pineapple juice, corn syrup, and ginger. Measure ham drippings. Add enough water to drippings to equal 1½ cups liquid; stir into mustard mixture. Micro-cook, uncovered, on 100% (*HIGH*) 2 to 5 minutes or until slightly thickened and clear, stirring after 2 minutes and then every minute. Spread over ham. Micro-cook glazed ham on 100% (*HIGH*) 8 to 13 minutes or until internal temperature reaches 130°. Remove from oven; cover ham loosely with foil and let stand 10 minutes. Makes 10 to 12 servings.

Microwave Thermometers

Do not use conventional meat thermometers inside the microwave oven. If a microwave thermometer or probe is unavailable, check ham outside the oven with a conventional meat thermometer, allowing 1 minute for temperature to register. Remove thermometer before continuing to micro-cook.

GERMAN POTATO SALAD AND BOLOGNA

3 cups thinly sliced potatoes	¼ teaspoon celery seed
½ teaspoon salt	¼ teaspoon dried parsley flakes
¼ cup water	Dash pepper
2 slices bacon, cut into eighths	½ cup water
½ cup chopped onion	¼ cup vinegar
1 tablespoon all-purpose flour	5 or 6 radishes, thinly sliced
1 tablespoon sugar	1 1-pound ring bologna, skinned and sliced into ½-inch-thick pieces
½ teaspoon salt	

In a 2-quart casserole place potatoes. Sprinkle with ½ teaspoon salt; pour ¼ cup water over all. Micro-cook, covered, on 100% (*HIGH*) 8 to 12 minutes or until potatoes are fork-tender, stirring after half the time. Set aside.

In a 4-cup measure micro-cook bacon, uncovered, on 100% (*HIGH*) 2 minutes. Add onion. Micro-cook, uncovered, on 100% (*HIGH*) for 1 to 3 minutes or until tender. Blend in flour, sugar, ½ teaspoon salt, the celery seed, parsley flakes, and pepper. Slowly stir in ½ cup water and the vinegar. Micro-cook, uncovered, on 100% (*HIGH*) 4 to 7 minutes or until thickened and clear, stirring after half the time.

Drain potatoes; add radishes and bologna. Pour vinegar mixture over all. Stir gently. Micro-cook, covered, on 100% (*HIGH*) 3 to 5 minutes or until bologna is heated through. Makes 2 to 4 servings.

SPICY SAUSAGE CASSEROLE

1 12-ounce package bulk pork sausage	½ teaspoon dried basil, crushed
½ cup finely chopped green pepper	¼ teaspoon dried thyme, crushed
½ cup finely chopped onion	¼ teaspoon pepper
1 16-ounce can whole tomatoes, cut up	⅛ teaspoon ground sage
¼ cup chili sauce	1¼ cups Minute Rice
½ teaspoon salt	1 cup shredded mozzarella cheese (4 ounces)

In a 1½- to 2-quart casserole crumble sausage. Add green pepper and onion. Micro-cook, uncovered, on 100% (*HIGH*) 4 to 6 minutes or until sausage is no longer pink, stirring once or twice. Drain; place sausage mixture on 2 or 3 layers of paper toweling and set aside. In same casserole combine tomatoes, chili sauce, salt, basil, thyme, pepper, and sage. Micro-cook, covered, on 100% (*HIGH*) 4 to 5 minutes or until bubbly.

Stir in sausage mixture and rice. Micro-cook, covered, on 50% (*MEDIUM*) 3 to 5 minutes or until rice is tender. Stir. Top with cheese. Micro-cook, uncovered, on 50% (*MEDIUM*) 2 to 6 minutes or until cheese melts, rotating once or twice. Makes 4 servings.

Microwaving Potatoes

Potatoes are naturally moist and need only a minimum of water to micro-cook for maximum flavor and nutrition. Slicing them thinly shortens cooking time.

How to Insert a Microwave Meat Thermometer in Leg of Lamb

The best way to test lamb for doneness is to check its internal temperature. If you have a microwave meat thermometer, insert it so the tip is in the center of the meaty area below the joint and does not touch the bone.

Do not use a conventional meat thermometer inside the microwave oven.

MARINATED LEG OF LAMB

1 **5-pound leg of lamb**	¼ **cup Worcestershire sauce**
⅓ **cup dry red wine**	3 **cloves garlic, minced**
¼ **cup cooking oil**	

Remove all excess fat from lamb. Place lamb in a large heavy plastic bag. Place bag in a large bowl. Combine wine, oil, Worcestershire, and garlic. Pour into bag. Close bag; chill several hours or overnight to marinate, turning bag occasionally. Remove lamb from bag, reserving marinade. Place lamb, bone side up, on a microwave baking rack in a 12×7½×2-inch baking dish. Cover with waxed paper. Micro-cook on 100% (*HIGH*) 5 minutes. Reduce power to 50% (*MEDIUM*) and micro-cook 20 minutes, rotating dish a half-turn after 10 minutes. Turn lamb over; brush with some of the marinade. Cover and micro-cook on 50% (*MEDIUM*) 30 to 40 minutes or till internal temperature reaches 140°, rotating dish a half-turn after 15 minutes. Cover with foil; let stand 10 minutes before carving. Makes 6 to 8 servings.

MARINATED LAMB KEBABS

¼ **cup soy sauce**	1 **medium green pepper,**
¼ **cup water**	**cut into 1½-inch pieces**
2 **teaspoons sugar**	2 **medium onions, cut into**
1 **teaspoon lemon juice**	**eighths**
¼ **teaspoon dried basil,**	8 **bamboo skewers, each**
crushed	**about 6 inches long**
1 **pound boneless lamb, cut**	¼ **cup water**
into 1-inch cubes	1 **tablespoon cornstarch**
1 **8¼-ounce can pineapple**	2 **teaspoons honey**
chunks	

In a 1-quart casserole or bowl combine soy sauce, ¼ cup water, sugar, lemon juice, and basil; add meat. Cover and marinate at room temperature 1 hour.

Drain meat, reserving ¼ cup marinade. Drain pineapple, reserving ¼ cup liquid. Make kebabs by alternating lamb cubes, pineapple chunks, green pepper pieces, and onion wedges on skewers. Place kebabs crosswise in a 12×7½×2-inch baking dish. Set aside.

For glaze, in a small bowl combine the reserved ¼ cup marinade, reserved ¼ cup pineapple liquid, ¼ cup water, cornstarch, and honey. Micro-cook, uncovered, on 100% (*HIGH*) 1½ to 3½ minutes or until thickened, stirring once or twice to blend.

Brush kebabs with ⅓ of the glaze; turn the kebabs over and brush with another ⅓ of the glaze. Cover dish with waxed paper. Micro-cook on 100% (*HIGH*) 8 minutes, rotating dish a half-turn after 4 minutes. Brush with remaining glaze.

Cover with waxed paper. Micro-cook on 50% (*MEDIUM*) 9 to 15 minutes or until meat is tender and vegetables are crisp-tender. Makes 4 servings.

LAMB CHOPS WITH WINE MARINADE

1 **cup dry white wine**	6 **lamb leg sirloin chops,**
¼ **cup sliced green onion**	**cut 1 inch thick**
1 **clove garlic, minced**	½ **cup water**
2 **teaspoons dry mustard**	1 **tablespoon cornstarch**
½ **teaspoon salt**	1 **teaspoon instant chicken**
½ **teaspoon pepper**	**bouillon granules**

For marinade, in a 12×7½×2-inch baking dish combine wine, onion, garlic, mustard, salt, and pepper. Place lamb chops in marinade, turning once to coat. Cover and marinate in refrigerator 1½ to 2 hours, turning chops once or twice. Micro-cook chops in marinade, uncovered, on 100% (*HIGH*) 5 minutes. Rotate dish a half-turn. Reduce power to 50% (*MEDIUM*). Micro-cook, uncovered, 8 minutes. Drain off marinade and reserve ¾ cup. Set aside. Turn chops over and rearrange so that least-cooked portions are toward outside of dish. Micro-cook, uncovered, on 50% (*MEDIUM*) 1 to 6 minutes or to desired doneness. Cover and keep warm. In a 4-cup measure blend water, cornstarch, and bouillon granules; stir in reserved ¾ cup marinade. Micro-cook on 100% (*HIGH*) 4 to 5 minutes or till thickened and bubbly, stirring every minute. Serve sauce with chops. Garnish chops with additional sliced green onion, if desired. Makes 3 to 4 servings.

LAMB-CABBAGE STEW

1 **pound lamb stew meat,**	¼ **teaspoon dried thyme,**
cut into ½-inch cubes	**crushed**
2 **cups hot water**	⅛ **teaspoon pepper**
1 **large onion, sliced and**	2 **cups shredded cabbage**
separated into rings	2 **medium tomatoes, peeled**
1 **clove garlic, minced**	**and cut into chunks**
2 **teaspoons instant beef**	½ **cup Minute Rice**
bouillon granules	1 **to 2 tablespoons lemon**
½ **teaspoon salt**	**juice**
¼ **teaspoon dried rosemary,**	
crushed	

In a 3-quart casserole combine lamb, water, onion, garlic, bouillon granules, salt, rosemary, thyme, and pepper. Micro-cook, covered, on 100% (*HIGH*) 5 minutes. Reduce power to 50% (*MEDIUM*). Micro-cook, covered, 20 minutes, stirring after 10 minutes.

Add cabbage, tomatoes, rice, and lemon juice. Micro-cook, covered, on 50% (*MEDIUM*) 20 to 25 minutes or until meat and vegetables are tender and flavors are blended. Let stand 5 minutes. Season to taste with additional salt and pepper, if desired. Makes 4 to 6 servings.

How to Identify Leg Sirloin Chops

Lamb leg sirloin chops are cut from the sirloin portion of the leg. They contain a crosscut of hip bone, which varies in shape and is located to one side of the chop.

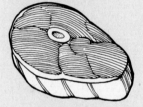

Lamb leg chops or steaks are cut from the shank portion, and contain a round crosscut of leg bone.

POULTRY

Poultry is one of our best proteins. It's nutritious, economical, and low in calories and cholesterol. Microwaving makes poultry even better because it extracts more fat, yet cooks the meat tender, flavorful, and juicy in minutes.

HAM AND SWISS CHICKEN ROLL-UPS WITH WINE SAUCE

½ cup fine dry bread crumbs	4 thin slices fully cooked ham
1 tablespoon grated Parmesan cheese	4 thin slices Swiss cheese
1 teaspoon dried snipped chives	2 tablespoons butter *or* margarine
1 teaspoon dried parsley flakes	2 tablespoons all-purpose flour
⅛ teaspoon poultry seasoning	1 teaspoon instant chicken bouillon granules
⅛ teaspoon celery seed	1 teaspoon dried parsley flakes
3 tablespoons butter *or* margarine	¼ teaspoon garlic powder
4 whole chicken breasts, skinned and boned	¼ teaspoon white pepper
	1 cup milk
	¼ cup dry white wine

In a pie plate combine bread crumbs, Parmesan cheese, chives, 1 teaspoon dried parsley, poultry seasoning, and celery seed. In a small bowl micro-cook 3 tablespoons butter or margarine, uncovered, on 100% (*HIGH*) 30 to 60 seconds or till melted. Brush inside of each chicken breast with melted butter or margarine. Place 1 slice *each* of ham and Swiss cheese on buttered side of each chicken breast and fold breast in half, folding cheese and ham as necessary to fit inside chicken breast. Brush outside with remaining melted butter and roll in crumb mixture to coat. Place breasts in a 12×7½×2-inch baking dish. Sprinkle *half* of the remaining crumbs over all. Micro-cook, uncovered, on 50% (*MEDIUM*) 10 minutes. Turn breasts over and sprinkle with remaining crumbs. Micro-cook, uncovered, on 50% (*MEDIUM*) 10 to 15 minutes or till meat is fork-tender, rotating a half-turn after 6 minutes. Keep warm.

For wine sauce, in a 4-cup measure micro-cook 2 tablespoons butter, uncovered, on 100% (*HIGH*) 30 to 50 seconds or till melted. Stir in flour, bouillon granules, 1 teaspoon parsley flakes, garlic powder, and white pepper. Mix well. Stir in milk and wine. Micro-cook, uncovered, on 100% (*HIGH*) 4 to 6 minutes or till thickened, stirring 3 or 4 times. Serve wine sauce over chicken breasts. Makes 4 servings.

How to Bone a Chicken Breast

Remove skin with your fingers.

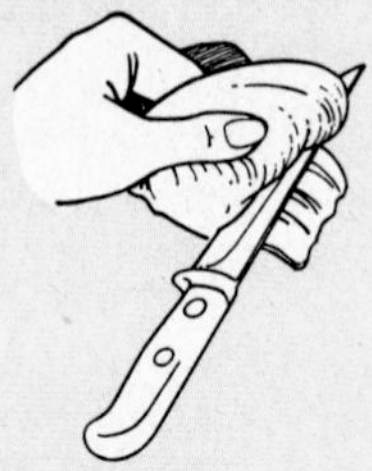

Cut against the breastbone on one side to loosen meat. Keeping the sharp edge of the knife angled toward the bones, cut against the ribs. Pull away the meat that you cut. Repeat on the other side of the breast.

CHICKEN BREASTS IN CREAM SAUCE

1 tablespoon butter *or* margarine	⅛ teaspoon dried thyme, crushed
2 whole large chicken breasts, skinned, boned, and halved lengthwise	⅛ teaspoon pepper
	⅛ teaspoon paprika
	¾ cup whipping cream
	⅓ cup dry white wine
2 tablespoons butter *or* margarine	1½ teaspoons dried parsley flakes
2 tablespoons all-purpose flour	Hot cooked rice (optional)
1 teaspoon instant chicken bouillon granules	

In an 8×8×2-inch baking dish micro-cook 1 tablespoon butter or margarine, uncovered, on 100% (*HIGH*) 30 to 60 seconds or until melted. Roll chicken in the melted butter and arrange in dish. Cover with waxed paper. Micro-cook on 100% (*HIGH*) 3 minutes; turn chicken over and micro-cook 3 minutes more. Set aside.

In a 2-cup measure micro-cook 2 tablespoons butter or margarine, uncovered, on 100% (*HIGH*) 45 to 60 seconds or until melted. Stir in flour, chicken bouillon granules, thyme, pepper, and paprika. Slowly blend in cream and wine; pour over chicken. Sprinkle with parsley flakes. Micro-cook, uncovered, on 100% (*HIGH*) 6 to 12 minutes or until sauce is thickened and chicken is tender, rearranging chicken and stirring sauce every 2 or 3 minutes. Serve over hot cooked rice, if desired. Makes 4 servings.

HAWAIIAN CHICKEN

1 2½- to 3-pound broiler-fryer chicken, cut up	½ cup catsup
⅓ cup packed brown sugar	⅓ cup raisins
1 tablespoon cornstarch	⅓ cup chopped walnuts
1 8¼-ounce can crushed pineapple	¼ cup chopped green onion
	2 tablespoons soy sauce

In a 12×7½×2-inch baking dish arrange chicken, skin side down, with meatiest portions toward outside of dish. Cover with waxed paper. Micro-cook on 100% (*HIGH*) 9 minutes, rotating dish a half-turn every 4 minutes. Meanwhile, in a medium bowl blend brown sugar and cornstarch. Stir in *undrained* pineapple, catsup, raisins, walnuts, green onion, and soy sauce. Drain chicken and turn skin side up. Pour soy mixture evenly over chicken. Cover with waxed paper. Micro-cook on 100% (*HIGH*) 10 to 11 minutes or until tender, bastinig and rotating dish a half-turn after half the cooking time. Makes 4 servings.

BARBECUED CHICKEN

½ cup catsup
¼ cup hot water
2 tablespoons prepared
  mustard
2 tablespoons Worcester-
  shire sauce
2 tablespoons dark
  molasses
1 tablespoon finely
  chopped onion

2 teaspoons instant chick-
  en bouillon granules
¼ teaspoon dried basil,
  crushed
¼ teaspoon garlic salt
3 drops bottled hot pepper
  sauce
1 2½- to 3-pound broiler-
  fryer chicken, cut up

In a 1-quart bowl or 4-cup measure combine catsup, hot water, mustard, Worcestershire sauce, molasses, onion, bouillon granules, basil, garlic salt, and hot pepper sauce. Micro-cook, uncovered, on 100% (*HIGH*) 4 to 6 minutes to heat and blend flavors, stirring every 2 minutes.

In a 12×7½×2-inch baking dish arrange chicken with the meatiest portions toward outside of dish. Pour sauce evenly over chicken. Cover with waxed paper. Micro-cook on 100% (*HIGH*) 10 minutes. Turn chicken over and rearrange so least-cooked portions are toward outside of dish. Re-cover with waxed paper. Micro-cook on 100% (*HIGH*) 10 to 16 minutes or until tender. Place chicken on a serving platter. Spoon excess fat from sauce. Pass sauce with chicken. Makes 4 to 6 servings.

COQ AU VIN

4 slices bacon, cut into
  1-inch pieces
1 2½- to 3-pound broiler-
  fryer chicken, cut up
2 cups sliced fresh
  mushrooms
1 medium onion, thinly
  sliced and separated
  into rings

¼ cup all-purpose flour
1 teaspoon salt
¼ teaspoon pepper
¼ teaspoon poultry
  seasoning
¼ teaspoon garlic powder
1 cup dry red wine
2 tablespoons snipped
  parsley

In a 3-quart casserole micro-cook bacon, covered, on 100% (*HIGH*) 3 to 5 minutes or until cooked, stirring after 2 minutes. Drain off fat, reserving 2 tablespoons in casserole. Set bacon aside. Place chicken in casserole. Sprinkle mushrooms and onion evenly over chicken.

In a mixing bowl combine flour, salt, pepper, poultry seasoning, and garlic powder. Slowly stir in red wine. Pour mixture over chicken; cover. Micro-cook on 100% (*HIGH*) 15 minutes, stirring and rotating bowl a half-turn after half the time. Stir sauce and rearrange chicken so that least-cooked portions are toward outside of dish. Micro-cook, uncovered, on 100% (*HIGH*) 5 to 15 minutes or until meat is tender, stirring every 5 minutes. Skim off any excess fat. Stir in parsley and cooked bacon. Cover and let stand 5 to 10 minutes. Makes 4 to 6 servings.

Skin Chicken to Reduce Calories

Most of a chicken's fat is located in, or directly under, the skin. If desired, the skin and excess fat can be removed before microwaving, since the meat will not stick to the dish during cooking. Cook in a sauce to give the chicken flavor and an attractive appearance.

CHICKEN PARMESAN

⅔ cup finely crushed rich
   round crackers
⅓ cup grated Parmesan
   cheese
1 tablespoon sesame seed
½ teaspoon garlic salt

½ teaspoon paprika
3 tablespoons butter or
   margarine
1 2½- to 3-pound broiler-
   fryer chicken, cut up
   and breast split
   lengthwise

In a 9-inch pie plate combine crushed crackers, cheese, sesame seed, garlic salt, and paprika. In a small dish micro-cook butter or margarine, uncovered, on 100% (HIGH) 30 to 50 seconds or until melted.

Brush chicken pieces with butter or margarine and roll in cracker mixture. Place chicken, bone side down, on a microwave baking rack in a 12×7½×2-inch baking dish; arrange meatiest portions toward outside of dish. Micro-cook, uncovered, on 100% (HIGH) 10 minutes. Rotate dish a half-turn. Micro-cook 4 to 10 minutes more or until chicken is tender. Makes 4 to 6 servings.

CURRIED CHICKEN

2 whole chicken breasts,
   skinned and boned
1 cup hot water
1 tablespoon instant chick-
   en bouillon granules
¼ cup butter or margarine
1 large onion, chopped
   (about 1 cup)

1 to 2 tablespoons curry
   powder
⅛ teaspoon white pepper
½ cup light cream
3 tablespoons all-purpose
   flour
   Slivered almonds
   (optional)

In a 2-quart casserole place chicken, hot water, and bouillon granules. Micro-cook, covered, on 100% (HIGH) 6 to 9 minutes or until meat is fork-tender, stirring once during cooking. Remove meat from broth; cut into bite-size pieces.

Add butter or margarine and onion to broth. Micro-cook, uncovered, on 100% (HIGH) 4 to 7 minutes or until butter is melted and onion is cooked, stirring after 3 minutes. Stir in curry powder and white pepper; stir in cream. Gradually blend in flour with a wire whisk. Micro-cook, uncovered, on 50% (MEDIUM) 5 to 9 minutes or until thickened, stirring every 3 minutes. Stir in cut-up chicken; micro-cook, uncovered, on 50% (MEDIUM) 3 to 5 minutes or until heated through, stirring once. Garnish with slivered almonds, if desired. Makes 4 servings.

Rotate Crumb-Coated Chicken

Arrange coated chicken pieces with the most attractive side up. Rotate the dish during micro-cooking, but do not turn chicken over. This helps keep the crumbs crisp.

Micro-Cooking a One-Plate Meal

Foods that cook at the same power level in approximately the same amount of time can be combined to make a one-plate meal. In this recipe, the corn is cut into pieces and arranged around the chicken legs so all the food fits on the baking rack. Rotating the dish eliminates the need to rearrange and turn the foods.

DRUMSTICKS AND CORN-ON-THE-COB

½ cup soy sauce	8 chicken legs
2 tablespoons cooking oil	2 tablespoons butter *or*
2 tablespoons honey	margarine
1 tablespoon lemon juice	2 teaspoons snipped chives
¼ teaspoon ground ginger	4 ears of corn, cut into
⅛ teaspoon garlic powder	4-inch pieces

In a medium bowl combine soy sauce, oil, honey, lemon juice, ginger, and garlic powder. If desired, remove skin from chicken legs. Add chicken legs to soy mixture; turn to coat. Cover and refrigerate 12 hours or overnight, turning legs several times. In a small bowl micro-cook butter or margarine on 100% (*HIGH*) about 45 seconds or till melted; add chives.

Place corn pieces around edges of a 12×7½×2-inch baking dish with microwave baking rack. Drain chicken legs. Arrange legs in center of rack, alternating meaty and bone ends for a closer fit. Brush corn with butter mixture. Cover dish with vented clear plastic wrap. Micro-cook on 100% (*HIGH*) 12 to 16 minutes or until chicken and corn are tender, rotating dish a quarter-turn twice during cooking. Let stand covered 5 minutes. Makes 4 servings.

CHICKEN WITH SAFFRON SAUCE

1 2½- to 3-pound broiler-fryer chicken, cut up	2 teaspoons dried parsley flakes
2 tablespoons sliced green onion	⅛ teaspoon saffron, finely crushed
2 tablespoons butter *or* margarine	¾ cup dry white wine
1 tablespoon instant chicken bouillon granules	¾ cup water
	3 tablespoons all-purpose flour
	Hot cooked rice

Arrange chicken pieces in a 12×7½×2-inch baking dish with meatiest pieces toward outside of dish. Cover with waxed paper. Micro-cook on 100% (*HIGH*) 10 minutes, rotating dish a half-turn after 5 minutes. Drain and discard fat and juices. Rearrange chicken so that least-cooked pieces are toward outside of dish.

In a 4-cup measure combine green onion, butter or margarine, chicken bouillon granules, parsley flakes, and saffron; stir in wine and ½ *cup* of the water. Micro-cook, uncovered, on 100% (*HIGH*) 1 minute. Pour over chicken; cover and micro-cook on 100% (*HIGH*) 8 to 10 minutes or till chicken is tender. Remove chicken to a serving platter; keep warm. Combine the remaining ¼ cup water and the flour. Add to mixture in dish; stir. Cook, uncovered, on 100% (*HIGH*) 3 to 4 minutes or till mixture is thickened and bubbly; stir frequently. Serve with chicken and hot cooked rice. Makes 4 servings.

CHICKEN TERIYAKI

1 2½- to 3-pound broiler-fryer chicken
½ cup soy sauce
2 tablespoons dry sherry
2 tablespoons sliced green onion
1 tablespoon brown sugar
1 clove garlic, minced
½ teaspoon grated fresh gingerroot

Wash and dry chicken; prick all over with a sharp fork. Place in a clear plastic bag in a 12×7½×2-inch baking dish. Combine soy sauce, sherry, green onion, brown sugar, garlic, and gingerroot; pour over chicken. Seal bag. Refrigerate overnight, turning bag over occasionally.

Drain chicken; place chicken, breast side down, on a microwave baking rack in the baking dish. Micro-cook, covered, on 100% (HIGH) 5 minutes. Reduce power to 50% (MEDIUM). Micro-cook, covered, 15 minutes, rotating dish after half the time. Turn chicken breast side up; cover. Micro-cook on 50% (MEDIUM) 10 to 20 minutes or till chicken is done, turning dish once. Makes 4 servings.

SOUP-SAUCED CHICKEN

1 2½- to 3-pound broiler-fryer chicken, cut up
1 10¾-ounce can condensed cream of chicken soup
1 4-ounce can mushroom stems and pieces
½ cup sliced almonds
2 tablespoons dry white wine
1 tablespoon Worcestershire sauce
1 teaspoon dried parsley flakes
½ teaspoon snipped chives
¼ teaspoon celery seed
1 10¾-ounce can condensed chicken broth
¼ cup all-purpose flour
   Hot cooked rice or noodles

In a 12×7½×2-inch baking dish arrange chicken with meatiest portions toward outside of dish. Combine chicken soup, undrained mushrooms, almonds, wine, Worcestershire sauce, parsley flakes, chives, and celery seed; spoon evenly over the chicken. Cover with waxed paper. Micro-cook on 100% (HIGH) 10 minutes. Turn chicken over and rearrange so least-cooked portions are toward outside of dish. Cover with waxed paper. Micro-cook on 100% (HIGH) 10 to 16 minutes or until tender. Remove chicken and cover with foil to keep warm; set aside.

Combine chicken broth and flour; stir into soup mixture. Micro-cook, uncovered, on 100% (HIGH) 8 to 12 minutes or until thickened, stirring every 3 minutes. Arrange chicken on a bed of rice or noodles; pour sauce over all. Makes 4 servings.

Microwaving a Whole Chicken

Chicken pieces micro-cook well on 100% (HIGH) power, but a whole chicken will cook more evenly if you reduce the power to 50% (MEDIUM) after the first 5 minutes. Whole chickens turn a light golden color when micro-cooked, but the teriyaki marinade in this recipe acts as a browning agent and provides deeper color.

Testing a Whole Chicken for Doneness

A whole chicken is done when the legs move freely and the juices run clear when the inner thigh is pierced with a fork or skewer. If you check the internal temperature with a meat thermometer, do so outside the oven, and allow 1 minute for an accurate reading. An automatic temperature probe should not be used when micro-cooking whole chicken because hot fat may run down the probe and cause the oven to turn off before the chicken is actually done.

CHICKEN WITH CRANBERRY GLAZE

3 tablespoons sugar	1½ teaspoons lemon juice
1 tablespoon cornstarch	2 tablespoons butter *or* margarine
½ cup cranberry-orange relish	2 tablespoons Worcester-shire sauce
½ cup cranberry juice cocktail	1 2½- to 3½-pound broiler-fryer chicken

For glaze, in a 4-cup measure combine sugar and cornstarch. Stir in cranberry-orange relish, cranberry juice, and lemon juice. Micro-cook, uncovered, on 100% (*HIGH*) 3 to 5 minutes or till thickened and bubbly, stirring twice. Set aside in a warm place.

In a small bowl or 1-cup measure heat butter or margarine at 100% (*HIGH*) 30 seconds or till melted; add Worcestershire sauce. Wash and dry chicken; brush skin with butter mixture. Place chicken, breast side down, in a 12×7½×2-inch baking dish. Cover and micro-cook on 100% (*HIGH*) 3 minutes. Reduce power to 50% (*MEDIUM*). To complete cooking allow 8 to 12 minutes per pound. Micro-cook, covered, on 50% (*MEDIUM*) the first half of the cooking time. Drain fat. Turn chicken breast side up. Micro-cook, covered, on 50% (*MEDIUM*) about 10 minutes. Uncover and spread half of the cranberry glaze over chicken. Continue cooking till legs move easily and chicken is done (185° internal temperature). Remove chicken to a platter; serve with remaining glaze. Makes 4 servings.

CHICKEN CACCIATORE

1 2½- to 3-pound broiler-fryer chicken, cut up	2 teaspoons dried parsley flakes
1 cup chopped green pepper	1½ teaspoons dried oregano, crushed
1 cup sliced fresh mushrooms	½ teaspoon salt
½ cup chopped onion	½ teaspoon garlic powder
1 16-ounce can tomatoes, cut up	¼ teaspoon dried thyme, crushed
1 6-ounce can tomato paste	¼ teaspoon pepper
½ cup dry red wine	Hot cooked spaghetti
1 tablespoon instant chicken bouillon granules	½ cup cold water
	2 tablespoons all-purpose flour

Arrange chicken pieces in a 3-quart casserole; add green pepper, mushrooms, and onion. Combine *undrained* tomatoes, tomato paste, wine, chicken bouillon granules, parsley flakes, oregano, salt, garlic powder, thyme, and pepper. Pour over chicken and vegetables. Cover and micro-cook on 100% (*HIGH*) 10 to 25 minutes or till done. Rearrange chicken pieces after 10 minutes of cooking. Remove chicken to a warm platter of cooked spaghetti; keep warm. Combine water and flour. Add to sauce in casserole; mix well. Micro-cook, uncovered, on 100% (*HIGH*) 3 to 4 minutes, stirring twice. Pour some of the sauce over chicken and spaghetti; pass remaining. Makes 4 servings.

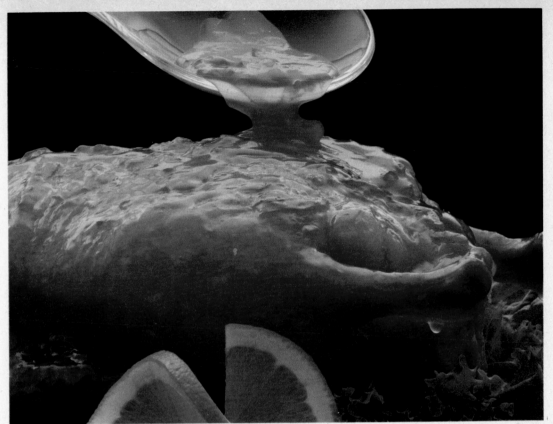

Duckling with Orange Sauce

DUCKLING WITH ORANGE SAUCE

1 4- to 5-pound domestic duckling	⅓ cup orange liqueur
⅓ cup orange juice	3 tablespoons soy sauce
3 tablespoons cornstarch	1 tablespoon lemon juice
1 18-ounce jar orange marmalade	1 tablespoon butter *or* margarine
	Orange slices

Remove and discard duckling giblets; wash duckling. Drain on paper toweling while preparing sauce.

For sauce, in a 4-cup measure combine orange juice and cornstarch. Stir in marmalade, liqueur, soy sauce, lemon juice, and butter or margarine. Micro-cook, uncovered, on 100% (*HIGH*) 4 to 7 minutes or until thickened and clear, stirring every 2 minutes. Set aside.

Place duckling, breast side down, on a microwave baking rack or inverted saucer in a 12×7½×2-inch baking dish. Twist wing tips under back. Micro-cook, uncovered, on 100% (*HIGH*) 10 minutes, rotating dish a half-turn after 5 minutes. Drain off fat. Reduce power to 50% (*MEDIUM*). Estimate remaining cooking time by allowing 4 to 7 minutes per pound. Micro-cook, uncovered, on 50% (*MEDIUM*) the first half of the remaining time. Drain fat from dish. Turn duckling breast side up. Spoon ⅓ of sauce over duckling. Micro-cook, uncovered, on 50% (*MEDIUM*) for the remaining time or until leg moves easily. Drain off fat. Pour another ⅓ of the sauce over duckling. Let stand tented with foil for 5 minutes. Garnish with orange slices. Serve remaining sauce with duckling. Makes 3 to 4 servings.

Microwaving Turkey

A 10-pound turkey is a convenient size for micro-cooking. The maximum size for a microwaved turkey is 12 to 14 pounds. Before cooking a bird of this larger size, test it for fit in your oven cavity. Turn it side to side as well as breast up and breast down. There should be at least 2 inches of space between the upper side of the turkey and the top of the oven.

TURKEY

1 10-pound frozen turkey, defrosted

Place turkey, breast side down, in a baking dish. Do not use a temperature probe (hot fat can run down the probe and turn the oven off before the turkey is done). Micro-cook, uncovered, on 100% (*HIGH*) 10 minutes. Reduce power to 50% (*MEDIUM*). Micro-cook, uncovered, 24 minutes, checking occasionally for areas that are browning too fast. (Shield these areas with foil as they occur and leave the shields on when turning the turkey.)

Turn turkey on its side. Micro-cook, uncovered, on 50% (*MEDIUM*) 34 minutes. Turn other side up. Micro-cook, uncovered, on 50% (*MEDIUM*) 34 minutes, basting and shielding turkey as needed.

Turn breast side up. Micro-cook, uncovered, on 50% (*MEDIUM*) 18 to 48 minutes or until drumstick moves freely at joint and flesh feels very soft when pressed. Internal temperature of meatiest part of thigh should register 185° after thermometer has been left in for 1 minute. Also, juices should run clear yellow when breast meat under wing is pierced with a skewer. Cover turkey loosely with foil and let stand 20 minutes. Makes 10 to 12 servings.

CORNISH HENS WITH PINEAPPLE STUFFING

¼ cup butter *or* margarine	½ cup sliced water chestnuts
⅓ cup chopped celery	
¼ cup chopped onion	2½ cups herb-seasoned stuffing croutons
1 tablespoon instant chicken bouillon granules	
	1 tablespoon butter *or* margarine
½ teaspoon poultry seasoning	1 tablespoon Kitchen Bouquet
2 slightly beaten eggs	4 1½-pound Cornish game hens
1 8¼-ounce can crushed pineapple	½ cup pineapple preserves

In a 2-quart bowl micro-cook ¼ cup butter or margarine, the celery, and onion, uncovered, on 100% (*HIGH*) 3 to 4 minutes or until tender. Stir in bouillon granules and poultry seasoning; add eggs, *undrained* pineapple, and water chestnuts. Stir in croutons; mix well.

In a small bowl combine 1 tablespoon butter or margarine and Kitchen Bouquet; micro-cook, uncovered, on 100% (*HIGH*) 20 to 60 seconds or until butter melts. Stuff hens with pineapple mixture. Arrange hens, breast side down, on a large nonmetal oven-going platter. Brush hens with some of the butter mixture. Cover with waxed paper. Micro-cook on 100% (*HIGH*) 15 minutes. Turn over and rearrange to move sides of hens that were toward edge of dish to the center; brush with remaining butter mixture. Micro-cook, covered, on 100% (*HIGH*) 13 to 20 minutes or until legs move easily and juices run clear. Immediately brush preserves over hens. Makes 4 servings.

GLAZED TURKEY BREAST

1 **8-pound fresh or frozen breast of turkey**	1 **tablespoon soy sauce**
½ **cup water**	1 **tablespoon honey**
⅓ **cup dry white wine**	1 **tablespoon cornstarch**

Defrost turkey, if frozen. Place turkey breast, skin side down, in a 12 × 7½ × 2-inch baking dish. Micro-cook, uncovered, on 100% (*HIGH*) 5 minutes. Reduce power to 50% (*MEDIUM*). Micro-cook, uncovered, 45 minutes. Turn skin side up. Micro-cook, uncovered, 40 to 70 minutes or until a thermometer inserted in meatiest part registers 170°. Let stand tented with foil 15 to 20 minutes.

Just before serving, combine water, wine, soy sauce, honey, and cornstarch in a small bowl. Micro-cook, uncovered, on 100% (*HIGH*) 2 to 3½ minutes or until thick and translucent, stirring with a wire whisk every minute. Brush glaze over turkey before serving. Makes 8 servings.

CORNISH HENS WITH CORN BREAD STUFFING

½ **cup chopped celery**	½ **cup hot water**
½ **cup chopped onion**	2 **teaspoons instant chicken bouillon granules**
¼ **cup butter or margarine**	
1½ **cups herb-seasoned stuffing croutons**	2 **beaten eggs**
3 **cups crumbled corn bread**	4 **1½-pound Cornish game hens**
1 **teaspoon poultry seasoning**	2 **tablespoons butter or margarine**
½ **teaspoon salt**	1 **teaspoon Kitchen Bouquet**
¼ **teaspoon pepper**	

In a large mixing bowl combine celery, onion, and ¼ cup butter or margarine. Micro-cook, uncovered, on 100% (*HIGH*) 2 to 4 minutes or until tender. Add croutons; toss to coat. Stir in crumbled corn bread. Add poultry seasoning, salt, and pepper; toss to coat. Combine hot water and bouillon granules; stir till dissolved. Stir bouillon and eggs into crouton mixture; mix well.

Rinse hens and pat dry. Sprinkle cavities with salt. Stuff hens with corn bread mixture. Place hens, breast side down, on a large nonmetal oven-going platter. In a small bowl micro-cook butter or margarine on 100% (*HIGH*) 30 to 60 seconds or until melted. Blend in Kitchen Bouquet. Brush each hen with some of the butter mixture. Cover with waxed paper. Micro-cook on 100% (*HIGH*) 20 minutes. Turn birds over and rearrange to move sides of hens that were toward edge of dish to the center. Brush with remaining butter mixture. Cover with waxed paper. Micro-cook on 100% (*HIGH*) 20 to 30 minutes or until legs move easily and juices run clear. Makes 4 servings.

How to Defrost a Turkey Breast

Place turkey breast, skin side down, on a microwave baking rack in a baking dish. Micro-cook, uncovered, on 50% (MEDIUM) 15 minutes. Shield warm spots with foil. Turn skin side up. Micro-cook, uncovered, on 50% (MEDIUM) 21 to 39 minutes. Let stand 5 to 10 minutes or until completely defrosted.

FISH & SHELLFISH

For fish and shellfish, many people prefer microwaving to conventional cooking. These delicate foods stay moist and tender with a minimum of very simple cooking.

SHRIMP-CHICKEN JAMBALAYA

4 slices bacon, cut into eighths	½ teaspoon sugar
1 medium green pepper, chopped	¼ teaspoon chili powder
1 medium onion, chopped	⅛ teaspoon pepper
1 16-ounce can tomatoes, cut up	⅛ teaspoon garlic powder
1 6-ounce can tomato paste	1 12-ounce package frozen shelled shrimp, thawed
½ cup water	1 cup cubed cooked chicken
2 teaspoons prepared mustard	1 6½-ounce can minced clams, drained
2 teaspoons Worcestershire sauce	Hot cooked rice
1 teaspoon salt	Bottled hot pepper sauce (optional)

Place bacon in a 2-quart casserole. Micro-cook, covered, on 100% (*HIGH*) 4 minutes. Drain, reserving 2 tablespoons drippings. Set bacon aside. Add green pepper and onion to drippings in casserole. Micro-cook, covered, on 100% (*HIGH*) 3½ to 5 minutes or until tender. Add *undrained* tomatoes, tomato paste, water, mustard, Worcestershire, salt, sugar, chili powder, pepper, and garlic powder. Micro-cook, covered, on 100% (*HIGH*) 5 minutes. Stir.

Reduce power to 50% (*MEDIUM*). Micro-cook, covered, 10 to 16 minutes or until thickened and bubbly, stirring once or twice. Add bacon, shrimp, chicken, and clams. Micro-cook, uncovered, on 50% (*MEDIUM*) 5 to 10 minutes or until shrimp are opaque, stirring once or twice. Cover; let stand 3 to 5 minutes. Serve over rice. If desired, pass hot sauce. Makes 4 servings.

Note: To thaw shrimp, separate shrimp; place in single layer in a baking dish. Micro-cook on 50% (*MEDIUM*) 3½ to 5 minutes or until defrosted, rearranging after half the time. Drain shrimp; pat dry.

COQUILLES ST. JACQUES

1 **pound fresh** *or* **frozen scallops**	¼ **teaspoon dried thyme, crushed**
8 **ounces fresh mushrooms, sliced**	3 **tablespoons butter**
⅓ **cup sliced green onion**	¼ **cup all-purpose flour**
⅓ **cup water**	¾ **cup light cream**
1 **tablespoon lemon juice**	¼ **cup dry white wine**
½ **teaspoon salt**	1 **tablespoon butter**
	¼ **cup fine dry bread crumbs**

Thaw scallops, if frozen. In a 2-quart casserole combine scallops, mushrooms, green onion, water, the lemon juice, salt, thyme, and ⅛ teaspoon *pepper*; cover. Micro-cook on 100% (*HIGH*) 7 to 8 minutes or until scallops are tender, stirring after half the cooking time. Drain well. In a 2-cup glass measure micro-cook the 3 tablespoons butter, uncovered, on 100% (*HIGH*) 30 to 60 seconds or until melted. Blend in flour until smooth. Slowly stir in light cream. Stir cream mixture into scallops. Micro-cook, uncovered, on 100% (*HIGH*) 3 to 6 minutes or until thickened, stirring every 2 minutes. Stir in ¼ cup wine. Let stand while preparing topping.

For topping, in a small bowl micro-cook 1 tablespoon butter, uncovered, on 100% (*HIGH*) 15 to 45 seconds or until melted. Stir in bread crumbs. Spoon scallop mixture into individual casseroles or baking shells. Sprinkle with crumb mixture. Micro-cook, uncovered, on 100% (*HIGH*) 1 to 2 minutes or until heated through, rotating once during cooking. Makes 4 servings.

SHRIMP CREOLE

1 **pound fresh** *or* **frozen medium shrimp in shells**	½ **cup dry red wine** *or* **water**
½ **cup chopped onion**	¼ **cup catsup**
½ **cup chopped green pepper**	1 **bay leaf**
½ **cup chopped celery**	1 **tablespoon dried parsley flakes**
1 **clove garlic, minced**	⅛ **teaspoon dried oregano, crushed**
2 **tablespoons olive oil** *or* **cooking oil**	⅛ **teaspoon dried thyme, crushed**
2 **teaspoons cornstarch**	**Dash cayenne**
1 **8-ounce can tomato sauce**	**Hot cooked rice**

Thaw shrimp, if frozen. Peel and devein shrimp. In a 1½- or 2-quart casserole combine onion, green pepper, celery, garlic, and olive oil. Micro-cook, uncovered, on 100% (*HIGH*) 3 to 5 minutes or until vegetables are tender, stirring after half the cooking time.

Stir in cornstarch until smooth. Stir in tomato sauce, red wine or water, catsup, bay leaf, parsley flakes, oregano, thyme, cayenne, ½ teaspoon *salt,* and dash *pepper.* Cover and micro-cook on 100% (*HIGH*) 3 minutes. Stir. Reduce power to 50% (*MEDIUM*). Micro-cook, uncovered, 8 to 15 minutes or until thickened and bubbly, stirring once or twice during cooking. Add shrimp. Micro-cook, uncovered, on 50% (*MEDIUM*) 4 to 7 minutes or until shrimp are opaque, stirring after half the cooking time. Cover and let stand 3 to 5 minutes. Serve over rice. Makes 4 servings.

Microwaving Shrimp

Shrimp are delicate; they toughen when over-cooked. When they are added to a hot sauce, they begin to cook immediately. To keep them tender, microwave on 50% (MEDIUM) just until they are opaque, then let them stand to complete cooking.

Stuffed Trout

STUFFED TROUT

2	6- to 8-ounce fresh *or* frozen dressed trout, boned	⅓	cup fine dry bread crumbs
2	tablespoons butter *or* margarine	1	teaspoon dried parsley flakes
¼	cup chopped onion	¼	teaspoon dried basil, crushed
¼	cup chopped celery	¼	teaspoon salt
¼	cup finely shredded carrot	⅛	teaspoon pepper
1	2-ounce can mushroom stems and pieces, drained	1	tablespoon butter *or* margarine
		1	teaspoon lemon juice

Thaw trout, if frozen. In a 1-quart casserole combine the 2 table-spoons butter or margarine, the onion, celery, and carrot. Micro-cook, uncovered, on 100% (*HIGH*) 2 to 3 minutes or until tender, stirring once. Stir in mushrooms, bread crumbs, parsley flakes, basil, salt, and pepper.

Place trout in a 12×7½×2-inch baking dish. Lightly pack half of the mushroom mixture into each trout, folding to close. In a small dish micro-cook 1 tablespoon butter or margarine, uncovered, on 100% (*HIGH*) 15 to 45 seconds or until melted. Stir in lemon juice. Brush fish with butter mixture; cover dish with waxed paper. Micro-cook on 100% (*HIGH*) 4 to 6 minutes or until fish flakes easily, rotating a half-turn after half the cooking time. Makes 2 servings.

How to Micro-Defrost Fish Fillets

Open package; if fillets can be separated, place them in the dish you will use to cook them later. Fish also may be thawed in the paper or plastic package. Defrost on 50% (MEDIUM) 3 to 5 minutes per pound. After half the time, separate, rearrange, or turn fish over. Defrost for remaining time, or until fish is pliable on the outside, but still icy in center of thick areas. Let stand 5 minutes, then rinse well.

HAWAIIAN FILLETS

1 **pound fresh *or* frozen fish fillets**
¼ **cup packed brown sugar**
1 **tablespoon cornstarch**
1 **8-ounce can pineapple chunks**
½ **medium green pepper, cut into thin strips**
¼ **cup vinegar**
1 **tablespoon soy sauce**
1 **teaspoon snipped chives**
   Dash garlic powder
¼ **cup sliced almonds, toasted**

Thaw fish, if frozen; cut fish into 4 serving-size pieces. In a 1-quart casserole combine brown sugar and cornstarch. Drain pineapple, reserving juice. Stir pineapple juice into brown sugar mixture. Stir in green pepper, vinegar, soy sauce, chives, and garlic powder. Micro-cook, uncovered, on 100% (*HIGH*) 2½ to 4½ minutes or until thickened, stirring every minute. Stir in pineapple chunks; set aside.

In a 2-quart casserole arrange fish, placing thicker portions toward outside of casserole; cover with waxed paper. Micro-cook on 100% (*HIGH*) 4 to 5 minutes or until fish flakes easily when tested with a fork, rotating dish a half-turn after half the cooking time. Drain well. Remove fish to a serving platter. Spoon pineapple mixture over fish. Sprinkle with toasted almonds. Makes 4 servings.

FISH IN WINE SAUCE

1 **pound fresh *or* frozen fish fillets**
2 **tablespoons butter *or* margarine**
2 **teaspoons minced dried onion**
2 **teaspoons dried parsley flakes**
¼ **teaspoon dried basil, crushed**
¼ **teaspoon salt**
⅓ **cup dry white wine**
¼ **cup water**
1 **tablespoon cold water**
1 **teaspoon cornstarch**

Thaw fish, if frozen. In a 12×7½×2-inch baking dish micro-cook butter or margarine, uncovered, on 100% (*HIGH*) 45 seconds to 1½ minutes or until melted. Stir in onion, parsley flakes, basil, and salt. Add wine and ¼ cup water. Arrange fillets in dish, turning once to coat. Cover dish with vented clear plastic wrap. Micro-cook on 100% (*HIGH*) 6 to 9 minutes or until fish flakes easily when tested with a fork; rearrange fish after half the cooking time. Remove fish and set aside.

Combine 1 tablespoon water and cornstarch. Stir into wine mixture. Micro-cook, uncovered, on 100% (*HIGH*) 2 to 3 minutes or until slightly thickened, stirring after each minute. Serve sauce with fish. Makes 4 servings.

CURRIED TUNA SHELLS

4 frozen patty shells	⅔ cup mayonnaise or salad
½ cup chopped celery	dressing
½ cup shredded carrot	¼ cup milk
¼ cup chopped onion	¼ cup slivered almonds
1 tablespoon butter or	¼ cup raisins
margarine	½ teaspoon salt
1 6½-ounce can tuna,	½ teaspoon curry powder
drained and flaked	Dash pepper
2 hard-cooked eggs,	
chopped	

Bake patty shells as directed on package; set aside. In a 1½-quart casserole combine celery, carrot, onion, and butter or margarine. Micro-cook, uncovered, on 100% (HIGH) 2½ to 3½ minutes or until vegetables are crisp-tender, stirring once.

Stir in tuna, eggs, mayonnaise or salad dressing, milk, almonds, raisins, salt, curry powder, and pepper. Micro-cook, uncovered, on 100% (HIGH) 3 to 3½ minutes or until heated through, stirring after half the cooking time. Place each patty shell on an individual serving plate. Spoon tuna mixture into shells, allowing excess to drape down sides of shell. Makes 4 servings.

TUNA-NOODLE CASSEROLE

1 3-ounce can french-fried	1 cup thinly sliced celery
onions	¾ cup milk
2 6½-ounce cans tuna,	½ cup dairy sour cream
drained and flaked	½ teaspoon salt
1 10¾-ounce can con-	¼ teaspoon pepper
densed cream of celery	¼ teaspoon onion powder
soup	½ cup cashews or peanuts,
1 2-ounce jar diced	coarsely chopped
pimiento, drained	3 cups cooked noodles

In a 2-quart casserole combine half of the onions with the tuna, soup, pimiento, celery, milk, sour cream, salt, pepper, onion powder, and cashews or peanuts. Gently stir in cooked noodles. Micro-cook, uncovered, on 100% (HIGH) 8 to 11 minutes or until thoroughly heated, stirring after half the cooking time. Sprinkle the remaining onions over top. Micro-cook, uncovered, on 100% (HIGH) 1 to 1½ minutes to warm onions. Makes 4 to 6 servings.

Bake Patty Shells Conventionally

Patty shells need dry heat. They puff in a microwave oven, but do not form a crisp crust to hold their shape.

EGGS & CHEESE

Eggs and cheese add variety to menus. Use High power for quick, fluffy scrambled eggs or to melt a cheese topping. A Medium setting lets you microwave delicate omelets or quiches.

EGG AND VEGETABLE RING WITH CHEESE SAUCE

1½	cups cauliflower flowerets	2	tablespoons butter or margarine
1½	cups broccoli, cut into 1-inch pieces	2	tablespoons all-purpose flour
2	tablespoons butter or margarine	¼	teaspoon salt
6	large eggs	⅛	teaspoon pepper
⅓	cup milk	1	cup milk
2	tablespoons grated Parmesan cheese	1	cup shredded cheddar cheese
½	teaspoon onion powder		Paprika
½	teaspoon salt		Cherry tomatoes (optional)
⅛	teaspoon pepper		

In a 1½-quart casserole combine cauliflower, broccoli, and 2 tablespoons butter or margarine. Micro-cook, covered, on 100% (*HIGH*) 5 to 6 minutes or until crisp-tender, stirring once during cooking. Drain thoroughly. Push vegetables from center and place a small glass in middle of casserole.

Beat together eggs, ⅓ cup milk, the Parmesan cheese, onion powder, ½ teaspoon salt, and ⅛ teaspoon pepper. Pour evenly over vegetables. Micro-cook, uncovered, on 100% (*HIGH*) 4 to 6 minutes or until almost set, lifting outer edges with a rubber spatula several times during cooking and rotating dish, if necessary. Let stand 5 to 10 minutes.

To make cheese sauce, in a 4-cup measure micro-cook 2 tablespoons butter or margarine, uncovered, on 100% (*HIGH*) 30 to 50 seconds or until melted. Stir in flour, ¼ teaspoon salt, and ⅛ teaspoon pepper until smooth. Stir 1 cup milk into flour-butter mixture. Micro-cook, uncovered, on 100% (*HIGH*) 3 to 4 minutes or until thickened, stirring every minute. Immediately stir cheddar cheese into hot sauce until melted.

Remove glass from casserole. Remove egg ring to serving plate. Pour half of cheese sauce over ring; sprinkle with paprika. Serve with remaining sauce. Garnish with cherry tomatoes, if desired. Serves 2 to 4.

Microwaving Eggs

Egg yolks attract more microwave energy than whites because of their higher fat content. Unless they are beaten together, the yolk may toughen before the white is set. In this recipe, the eggs are mixed with milk and stirred several times during preliminary cooking before they are placed in the hash cups and micro-cooked until set.

EGGS AND HASH

1 **15-ounce can corned beef hash**	**Dash pepper**
4 **eggs**	¼ **cup shredded cheddar cheese**
3 **tablespoons milk**	½ **teaspoon snipped chives**
Dash salt	

In each of 4 custard cups place ¼ of hash. Spread hash evenly over bottoms and sides of cups. Set aside. In a 2-cup measure beat together eggs, milk, salt, and pepper. Micro-cook, uncovered, on 100% (*HIGH*) 2 to 3 minutes or until somewhat set but still very runny, stirring 2 or 3 times during cooking.

Place ¼ of egg mixture in each custard cup. Micro-cook, uncovered, on 100% (*HIGH*) 1½ minutes or until set. Sprinkle cheese and chives evenly over eggs and rearrange cups. Micro-cook, uncovered, on 100% (*HIGH*) 1½ to 2½ minutes or until cheese is melted and eggs are cooked. Makes 4 servings.

PINEAPPLE-ORANGE OMELET

2 **medium oranges**	**Puffy Omelet (see Puffy Omelet with Vegetable Filling, right)**
3 **tablespoons granulated sugar**	
2 **teaspoons cornstarch**	¼ **cup powdered sugar**
1 **8-ounce can pineapple chunks (juice pack)**	

For sauce, peel *1* of the oranges, removing membrane with the peel. Section orange and set aside. In a 2-cup measure combine granulated sugar and cornstarch. Drain pineapple juice into sugar mixture; stir until blended. Set aside pineapple chunks. Micro-cook the remaining orange on 100% (*HIGH*) 10 to 30 seconds or until just warm. Squeeze orange and remove any seeds; stir juice into sugar mixture. Micro-cook, uncovered, on 100% (*HIGH*) 2 to 3½ minutes or until sauce is thickened and shiny, stirring once or twice during cooking.

Prepare Puffy Omelet as directed, *except* omit basil. Arrange orange sections and pineapple chunks over one half of omelet; fold. Reheat sauce, if necessary; drizzle over omelet. Sift powdered sugar over top. Makes 2 servings.

PUFFY OMELET WITH VEGETABLE FILLING

Vegetable Filling
4 eggs, separated
¼ cup milk
½ teaspoon baking powder
½ teaspoon salt

⅛ teaspoon dried basil,
crushed
Dash pepper
1 tablespoon butter or
margarine
Dash salt

Prepare Vegetable Filling. For the omelet, in a small mixing bowl beat egg yolks till thick and lemon colored; stir in milk, baking powder, ½ teaspoon salt, the basil, and pepper. Set aside. In a medium mixer bowl, beat egg whites until stiff peaks form. Fold yolk mixture into egg whites. Set aside.

In a 9-inch pie plate micro-cook butter or margarine, uncovered, on 100% (*HIGH*) 30 to 45 seconds or until melted. Pour eggs into pie plate. Micro-cook, uncovered, on 50% (*MEDIUM*) 3 to 5 minutes or until partially set. Lift edges of omelet to allow uncooked portion to spread evenly over dish. Micro-cook, uncovered, on 100% (*HIGH*) 2½ to 4½ minutes or until center is almost set. Using a slotted spoon, spread Vegetable Filling over half of omelet. Sprinkle with dash salt. Loosen omelet with spatula and fold in half. Gently slide onto serving plate. Makes 2 servings.

Vegetable Filling: In a 1-quart casserole combine 1 cup sliced fresh *mushrooms;* 1 small *potato,* peeled and cut into ½-inch cubes; ¼ cup chopped *onion;* 2 teaspoons *olive oil or cooking oil;* ¼ teaspoon dried *parsley flakes;* and ¼ teaspoon *salt.* Micro-cook, covered, on 100% (*HIGH*) 3 to 5 minutes or till tender, stirring after half the time. Set aside.

SAUCY CHICKEN OMELET

1 tablespoon butter or
margarine
1 tablespoon all-purpose
flour
¼ teaspoon salt
⅛ teaspoon pepper
¾ cup light cream
1 cup diced cooked
chicken or turkey

1 tablespoon snipped
chives
1 tablespoon chopped
pimiento (optional)
Puffy Omelet (see Puffy
Omelet with Vegetable
Filling, above)

For sauce, in a medium bowl micro-cook butter or margarine, uncovered, on 100% (*HIGH*) 30 to 60 seconds or until melted. Stir in flour, salt, and pepper. Stir in cream. Micro-cook, uncovered, on 100% (*HIGH*) 2½ to 3 minutes or till thickened and bubbly, stirring every minute. Add chicken or turkey, chives, and pimiento, if desired. Micro-cook, uncovered, on 100% (*HIGH*) 1 to 3 minutes or until hot, stirring every minute. Prepare Puffy Omelet as directed, omitting the Vegetable Filling. Reheat sauce, if necessary; serve over omelet. Makes 2 to 4 servings.

Puffy Omelets

Microwaving puffy omelets saves energy as well as time, because you don't have to heat both the range top and the oven. Remove omelet from the microwave when the center is almost but not completely set.

The omelet will finish cooking from internal heat while you fill or sauce it.

Microwaving Two or More Sandwiches

A large browning dish or a browning grill will hold more than one sandwich and cook them in the same amount of time. If you have too many sandwiches to fit in the dish, preheat the browning utensil again for each batch.

GRILLED HAM AND CHEESE SANDWICH

Horseradish mustard	1 or 2 slices fully cooked
2 slices whole wheat bread	ham
2 slices American *or*	Butter *or* margarine
process Swiss cheese	

Preheat a microwave browning dish on 100% (*HIGH*) 5 minutes. (*Or,* preheat microwave browning grill 7 minutes.) Meanwhile, spread mustard on one side of bread slices; add 1 slice cheese, ham, and the remaining cheese. Top with bread. Butter outside of sandwich on both sides.

Place on preheated browning dish. Flatten slightly with spatula. Let stand 15 to 20 seconds. Turn sandwich over, flatten slightly. Let stand 20 to 25 seconds. Micro-cook, uncovered, on 100% (*HIGH*) 20 to 45 seconds to finish melting cheese. Makes 1.

COMPANY SCRAMBLED EGGS

½ pound bulk pork sausage	½ teaspoon salt
⅓ cup sliced green onion	½ teaspoon dry mustard
8 eggs	¼ teaspoon pepper
¼ cup dairy sour cream	1 cup shredded Swiss
¼ cup milk	cheese (4 ounces)

In an 8×1½-inch round baking dish, break up sausage. Micro-cook, uncovered, on 100% (*HIGH*) 3 to 5 minutes or until meat loses its pink color, stirring once during cooking. Drain sausage, reserving 2 tablespoons drippings; place sausage on paper toweling. Micro-cook green onion in reserved drippings in the baking dish, uncovered, on 100% (*HIGH*) 1 minute.

In a large mixing bowl combine eggs, sour cream, milk, salt, mustard, and pepper; pour over onion in baking dish. Micro-cook, uncovered, on 100% (*HIGH*) 5 to 7 minutes or until eggs are almost set, pushing cooked portions to center of dish several times during cooking. Top eggs with sausage; sprinkle with cheese. Micro-cook on 50% (*MEDIUM*) 3 to 6 minutes or until cheese is melted. Cut into wedges. Makes 6 servings.

CHEDDAR CHEESE FONDUE

½ cup beer	1 teaspoon dry mustard
4 cups shredded cheddar	Dash garlic powder
cheese (16 ounces)	¼ cup milk
3 tablespoons all-purpose	½ teaspoon Worcestershire
flour	sauce
	Vegetable dippers

In a 2-quart casserole micro-cook beer on 100% (*HIGH*) 5 seconds to 1 minute or until hot. Combine cheese, flour, dry mustard, and garlic powder. Add to beer with milk and Worcestershire sauce. Micro-cook, uncovered, on 50% (*MEDIUM*) 5 to 9 minutes or until cheese is melted, stirring well every 2 minutes. If desired, place in fondue pot over low heat to keep warm or reheat as necessary. Serve with vegetable dippers. Makes 4 to 8 servings.

SWISS FONDUE

1½ cups dry white wine	1 clove garlic, minced
4 cups shredded Swiss cheese (16 ounces)	⅛ teaspoon white pepper
5 teaspoons cornstarch	⅛ teaspoon nutmeg
	Bread cubes

In a 2-quart casserole micro-cook wine, uncovered, on 50% (*MEDIUM*) 4 to 8 minutes or until bubbles form (do not boil). Combine cheese, cornstarch, garlic, pepper, and nutmeg; add to wine. Micro-cook, uncovered, on 50% (*MEDIUM*) 4 to 8 minutes or until cheese is melted, stirring well every 2 minutes. Reheat as needed. If desired, place in fondue pot over low heat to keep warm. Serve with bread cubes for dipping. Makes 4 servings.

SPINACH-CHEESE CUSTARD

2 10-ounce packages frozen chopped spinach	4 beaten eggs
1 cup shredded American cheese (4 ounces)	1 cup milk
	1 tablespoon butter *or* margarine
¼ cup packaged biscuit mix	½ cup shredded American cheese (2 ounces)
¼ teaspoon garlic salt	
⅛ teaspoon pepper	

In a 1½-quart casserole place spinach. Micro-cook, covered, on 100% (*HIGH*) 5 minutes. Stir spinach to break up any icy portions. Micro-cook, covered, on 100% (*HIGH*) 3 to 4 minutes. Drain very well to remove all liquid. Combine spinach, 1 cup cheese, the biscuit mix, garlic salt, and pepper. Stir in eggs and milk until mixed.

In an 8×8×2-inch baking dish micro-cook butter or margarine, uncovered, on 100% (*HIGH*) 30 to 45 seconds or until melted. Tilt dish to coat bottom and sides. Pour in spinach mixture. Micro-cook, covered, on 100% (*HIGH*) 7 minutes, stirring after 3 minutes and again after another minute. Top with ½ cup cheese. Micro-cook, uncovered, on 100% (*HIGH*) 30 seconds. Serves 6.

DENVER SANDWICHES

¼ cup chopped green pepper	¾ cup cubed fully cooked ham
¼ cup chopped onion	1 tablespoon milk
1 tablespoon butter *or* margarine	Dash pepper
3 eggs	2 slices white bread, toasted

In a 2-cup measure combine green pepper, onion, and butter or margarine. Micro-cook, uncovered, on 100% (*HIGH*) 1½ to 2½ minutes or until tender. Blend in eggs, ham, milk, and pepper.

Divide mixture evenly between two microwave-safe saucers. Micro-cook, uncovered, on 100% (*HIGH*) 2 to 5 minutes or until almost set, pushing set portions to center of dish once or twice. (Egg mixture should remain shaped rather than scrambled.) Rotate saucers once or twice. Serve each portion of egg on a toast slice. Makes 2 servings.

Fondue Variety

Natural cheese microwaves with a slightly coarse texture. If you prefer a smooth fondue, select process cheese.

For a slightly more nippy flavor, substitute 2 cups (8 ounces) Gruyère for half of the Swiss cheese.

LEFTOVERS

Microwaved leftovers are so fresh-tasting, you won't mind serving them the second day. You also can create a variety of new main dishes, using these recipes and whatever you have on hand.

SWEET-SOUR MEAT AND VEGETABLES

1 8¼-ounce can pineapple chunks	2 cups cubed cooked pork, chicken, *or* ham (¾-inch cubes)
¼ cup soy sauce	
4 teaspoons cornstarch	1 cup fresh *or* canned bean sprouts
2 tablespoons brown sugar	
2 tablespoons vinegar	1 8-ounce can sliced water chestnuts, drained
¼ teaspoon ground ginger	
Dash garlic powder	1 4-ounce can mushroom stems and pieces, drained
1 medium green pepper, cut into 1-inch squares	
1 tablespoon butter *or* margarine	Chow mein noodles *or* hot cooked rice

Drain pineapple, reserving juice. Combine pineapple juice and soy sauce; add enough water to make 1 cup liquid. In a 4-cup measure blend soy mixture into cornstarch; stir in brown sugar, vinegar, ginger, and garlic powder. Micro-cook, uncovered, on 100% (*HIGH*) 3 to 5 minutes or until thickened, stirring several times during cooking. Set aside.

In a 2-quart casserole micro-cook green pepper and butter or margarine, uncovered, on 100% (*HIGH*) 2 to 4½ minutes or until crisp-tender. Stir in soy mixture, pineapple chunks, meat, bean sprouts, water chestnuts, and mushrooms. Micro-cook, covered, on 100% (*HIGH*) 2 minutes. Stir. Reduce power to 50% (*MEDI-UM*). Micro-cook 2 to 5 minutes or until heated through. Serve over chow mein noodles or rice. Makes 4 to 6 servings.

MEXICAN BEAN CASSEROLE

½ medium green pepper, chopped (about ⅓ cup)
1 tablespoon butter *or* margarine
1½ cups cubed cooked beef *or* pork (½-inch cubes)
1 15½-ounce can chili beans
1 6-ounce can tomato paste
¼ cup chopped pitted ripe olives
¼ cup water
¼ cup chili sauce
1 tablespoon chopped canned green chili peppers (optional)
½ teaspoon chili powder
¼ teaspoon salt
⅛ teaspoon crushed red pepper
½ cup dairy sour cream
1 egg
⅛ teaspoon pepper
2 cups broken tortilla chips
½ cup shredded Monterey Jack cheese (2 ounces)
½ cup shredded cheddar cheese (2 ounces)

In a 2-quart casserole micro-cook green pepper in butter or margarine, uncovered, on 100% (*HIGH*) 1½ to 2 minutes or until tender. Stir in beef or pork, *undrained* chili beans, tomato paste, olives, water, chili sauce, green chili peppers, chili powder, salt, and red pepper; cover. Micro-cook on 100% (*HIGH*) 5 minutes; stir. Reduce power to 50% (*MEDIUM*). Micro-cook, uncovered, 5 to 10 minutes or until thickened, stirring once or twice during cooking. Meanwhile, in a small bowl blend together sour cream, egg, and pepper. Spoon *half* of the meat mixture evenly into an 8×8×2-inch baking dish. Pour sour cream mixture over meat; top with remaining meat mixture. Top evenly with tortilla chips; sprinkle with Monterey Jack cheese and cheddar cheese. Micro-cook, uncovered, on 50% (*MEDIUM*) 4 to 5 minutes or until cheese melts, rotating once during cooking, if necessary. Let stand 3 to 5 minutes. Makes 4 servings.

MUSHROOM-SAUCED BEEF AND PEA PODS

1 6-ounce package frozen pea pods
2 cups thinly sliced cooked beef strips
1 10¾-ounce can condensed cream of mushroom soup
1 4-ounce can mushroom stems and pieces, drained
2 tablespoons dry sherry
1 tablespoon soy sauce
⅛ teaspoon ground ginger
⅛ teaspoon garlic powder
Chow mein noodles *or* hot cooked rice

Run cold water over frozen pea pods to separate.

In a 2-quart casserole combine pea pods, meat, soup, mushrooms, sherry, soy sauce, ginger, and garlic powder. Micro-cook, covered, on 100% (*HIGH*) 5 minutes. Stir. Micro-cook, covered, on 50% (*MEDIUM*) 6 to 10 minutes or until hot. Serve over chow mein noodles or rice. Makes 4 servings.

BEEF-VEGETABLE BAKE

1 **9-ounce package frozen cut green beans**	1 **4-ounce can mushroom stems and pieces, drained**
1 **cup chopped onion**	
1 **tablespoon butter** *or* **margarine**	1 **tablespoon soy sauce**
	½ **teaspoon salt**
2 **cups cubed cooked beef (½-inch cubes)**	⅛ **teaspoon pepper**
	3 **cups frozen loose-pack hashed brown potatoes**
1 **10¾-ounce can condensed cream of mushroom soup**	1 **cup shredded cheddar cheese (4 ounces)**
	¼ **teaspoon paprika**

Place opened package of beans on paper toweling in microwave oven. Micro-cook on 100% (*HIGH*) 3 to 4 minutes or until defrosted. Drain well; set aside. In a 2-quart casserole combine onion and butter or margarine. Micro-cook, uncovered, on 100% (*HIGH*) 2 to 3 minutes or until onion is tender.

Stir in beef, soup, mushrooms, soy sauce, salt, pepper, and green beans. Sprinkle hashed browns over top. Micro-cook, uncovered, on 100% (*HIGH*) 10 to 18 minutes or until heated through, rotating a half-turn after half the cooking time. Top evenly with cheese; sprinkle with paprika. Reduce power to 50% (*MEDIUM*). Micro-cook, covered, 2 to 5 minutes or until cheese melts. Makes 4 servings.

TOMATO MEAT SAUCE

1 **large onion, thinly sliced**	½ **cup dry red wine** *or* **beef broth**
1 **clove garlic, minced**	
1 **tablespoon olive oil** *or* **cooking oil**	2 **teaspoons brown sugar**
	1 **teaspoon salt**
2 **cups cubed cooked beef** *or* **pork (½-inch cubes)**	1 **teaspoon dried oregano, crushed**
1 **16-ounce can tomatoes, cut up**	1 **teaspoon dried basil, crushed**
1 **6-ounce can tomato paste**	⅛ **teaspoon pepper**
1 **4-ounce can mushroom stems and pieces, drained**	**Hot cooked noodles** *or* **spaghetti**
	Grated Parmesan cheese (optional)

In a 2-quart casserole combine onion, garlic, and oil; cover. Micro-cook on 100% (*HIGH*) 2 to 3 minutes or until tender. Add beef or pork, tomatoes, tomato paste, mushrooms, wine or broth, brown sugar, salt, oregano, basil, and pepper; cover. Micro-cook on 100% (*HIGH*) 5 minutes; stir. Reduce power to 50% (*MEDIUM*). Micro-cook, uncovered, 21 to 32 minutes or to desired thickness, stirring several times during cooking. Serve over noodles or spaghetti. Sprinkle with cheese, if desired. Makes 4 servings.

Rotate Layered Casseroles

Layered casseroles cannot be stirred during cooking because this would disturb the layers. Rotate these casseroles to help distribute heat evenly.

Stuffed Green Peppers

STUFFED GREEN PEPPERS

½	cup chopped celery	⅛	teaspoon garlic powder
½	cup chopped onion	1½	cups cubed cooked
1	tablespoon butter *or* margarine		beef, pork, *or* chicken (¼-inch cubes)
1	8-ounce can tomato sauce	2	large green peppers, halved lengthwise and seeds and core removed
¾	cup Minute Rice		
½	teaspoon salt		
¼	teaspoon sugar	½	cup shredded cheddar cheese (2 ounces) (optional)
¼	teaspoon dried basil, crushed		
¼	teaspoon pepper		

In a 1-quart casserole micro-cook celery, onion, and butter or margarine, covered, on 100% (*HIGH*) 2 to 4 minutes or until tender. Stir in tomato sauce, rice, salt, sugar, basil, pepper, and garlic powder. Micro-cook, covered, on 100% (*HIGH*) 2 to 4 minutes or until rice is tender. Stir in meat; cover. Set aside.

Place peppers cut side up in an 8×8×2-inch baking dish. Cover with vented clear plastic wrap. Micro-cook on 100% (*HIGH*) 1½ to 2½ minutes or until peppers are hot. Drain liquid from peppers. Mound meat mixture into pepper shells; cover. Micro-cook on 100% (*HIGH*) 1½ to 2½ minutes. Reduce power to 50% (*MEDI-UM*). Micro-cook, covered, 3 to 6 minutes or until mixture is hot and peppers are tender. If desired, sprinkle each with 2 table-spoons cheese. Cover and let stand 1 to 3 minutes. Makes 4 servings.

COOKED MEAT STEW

2 cups cubed cooked beef *or* pork (½-inch cubes)
1 16-ounce can tomatoes, cut up
1 cup frozen cut green beans
1 medium potato, peeled and cut into ½-inch cubes
1 medium onion, thinly sliced
⅔ cup hot water
1 bay leaf
2 teaspoons instant beef bouillon granules
1 teaspoon salt
½ teaspoon dried basil, crushed
⅛ teaspoon pepper
1 cup frozen peas and carrots
⅓ cup cold water
3 tablespoons all-purpose flour

In a 3-quart casserole combine beef or pork, *undrained* tomatoes, green beans, potato, onion, ⅔ cup hot water, bay leaf, bouillon granules, salt, basil, and pepper; cover. Micro-cook on 100% (*HIGH*) 10 minutes. Stir. Reduce power to 50% (*MEDIUM*). Micro-cook, covered, 15 minutes; stir in peas and carrots. Micro-cook, covered, 10 to 15 minutes or until potatoes and onion are tender. Blend ⅓ cup cold water and flour; stir into meat mixture. Cook, uncovered, on 100% (*HIGH*) 1 to 2 minutes or until thickened and bubbly, stirring three times. Remove bay leaf. Makes 4 to 6 servings.

SAUCY MEAT AND VEGETABLES

1 10-ounce package frozen French-style green beans
1 medium onion, chopped
1 tablespoon butter *or* margarine
2 cups cubed cooked beef, pork, *or* chicken (½-inch cubes)
1 10¾-ounce can condensed cream of mushroom soup
1 5⅓-ounce can evaporated milk
1 4-ounce can mushroom stems and pieces, drained
¼ teaspoon pepper
⅛ teaspoon ground nutmeg
Dash garlic powder
½ cup chopped peanuts

Place opened package of beans on paper toweling in microwave oven. Micro-cook on 100% (*HIGH*) 3 to 4 minutes or until defrosted. Drain well; set aside. In a 2-quart casserole combine onion and butter or margarine. Micro-cook, uncovered, on 100% (*HIGH*) 2 to 2½ minutes or until tender. Stir in meat, soup, milk, mushrooms, pepper, nutmeg, garlic powder, and beans; cover. Micro-cook on 100% (*HIGH*) 7 to 10 minutes or until heated through, stirring every 3 minutes. Sprinkle with peanuts. Makes 4 servings.

Small Pieces Reduce Cooking Time

Cut the potatoes in ½-inch cubes to speed cooking. Reducing the power to 50% (MEDIUM) after the first 10 minutes of cooking allows the potatoes to become tender without overcooking the leftover beef.

Hard-Cook Eggs Conventionally

Never try to hard-cook an egg in the microwave oven. Steam builds up inside the shell and causes it to burst. Whole, shelled, hard-cooked eggs should be cut up before they are added to casseroles for microwave heating.

CREAMY HAM AND ASPARAGUS

2 **hard-cooked eggs (see tip at left)**	2 **tablespoons all-purpose flour**
1 **10-ounce package frozen cut asparagus**	¼ **teaspoon salt**
1½ **cups fully cooked ham cut into strips**	⅛ **teaspoon pepper**
½ **cup shredded cheddar cheese (2 ounces)**	1 **cup milk**
2 **tablespoons butter *or* margarine**	¼ **teaspoon paprika**
	Toast points *or* toasted English muffin halves

Cut hard-cooked eggs into eighths; set aside. Place package of asparagus on paper toweling in oven. Micro-cook on 100% (*HIGH*) 3½ to 6 minutes or until defrosted. Drain well. In an 8×8×2-inch baking dish arrange asparagus to cover bottom. Top with ham strips and hard-cooked eggs; sprinkle with cheese. Set aside.

In a 4-cup measure micro-cook butter or margarine, uncovered, on 100% (*HIGH*) 30 to 60 seconds or until melted. Blend in flour, salt, and pepper. Slowly stir in milk. Micro-cook, uncovered, on 100% (*HIGH*) 3 to 4 minutes or until thickened, stirring every minute. Pour sauce evenly over ham mixture. Sprinkle paprika over sauce. Cover with vented clear plastic wrap. Micro-cook on 100% (*HIGH*) 2½ to 5 minutes or until heated through, rotating dish a half-turn after half the cooking time. Serve hot over toast points or toasted English muffins. Makes 4 servings.

LAMB OR PORK CURRY

1 **medium apple, cored and chopped**	1 **teaspoon lemon juice**
½ **cup chopped green pepper**	½ **teaspoon salt**
½ **cup chopped onion**	½ **teaspoon dried thyme, crushed**
2 **tablespoons butter *or* margarine**	2 **cups cubed cooked lamb *or* pork (¾-inch cubes)**
3 **tablespoons all-purpose flour**	1¼ **cups water**
2 to 2½ **teaspoons curry powder**	¼ **teaspoon Kitchen Bouquet**
1 **teaspoon instant chicken bouillon granules**	**Hot cooked rice**
	⅓ **cup chopped peanuts**

In a 2-quart casserole combine apple, green pepper, onion, and butter or margarine; cover. Micro-cook on 100% (*HIGH*) 3 to 4 minutes or until tender, stirring once during cooking.

Stir in flour, curry powder, bouillon granules, lemon juice, salt, and thyme. Add lamb or pork and water; cover. Micro-cook on 100% (*HIGH*) 3 minutes. Stir. Reduce power to 50% (*MEDIUM*). Micro-cook, uncovered, 10 to 18 minutes or until thickened and bubbly, stirring several times during cooking. Stir in Kitchen Bouquet. Serve over rice. Sprinkle with peanuts. Makes 4 servings.

LAMB PILAF

½ **cup chopped celery**	½ **teaspoon dried**
⅓ **cup chopped onion**	**marjoram, crushed**
1 **tablespoon olive oil** *or*	1 **bay leaf**
cooking oil	1½ **cups cubed cooked lamb**
1 **9-ounce package**	*or* **pork (¾-inch cubes)**
rice pilaf mix	⅓ **cup raisins**
1 **teaspoon snipped chives**	⅓ **cup sliced almonds**

In a 2-quart casserole combine celery, onion, and oil. Micro-cook, uncovered, on 100% (*HIGH*) 2 to 3 minutes or until tender. Stir in rice from pilaf mix and 2 cups hot *water*. Stir in seasoning packet from pilaf mix, chives, marjoram, and bay leaf; cover. Micro-cook on 100% (*HIGH*) 5 minutes. Reduce power to 50% (*MEDIUM*). Micro-cook 10 to 13 minutes or until rice is tender, stirring occasionally. Stir in lamb or pork and raisins. Micro-cook, covered, on 50% (*MEDIUM*) 3 to 5 minutes or until meat is hot, stirring once. Remove bay leaf. Stir in almonds. Makes 4 servings.

POULTRY DIVAN CASSEROLE

2 **10-ounce packages**	¼ **cup mayonnaise**
frozen chopped broccoli	2 **tablespoons dry white**
2 **cups cooked chicken** *or*	**wine**
turkey cut into strips	2 **tablespoons milk**
1 **10¾-ounce can con-**	**Dash garlic powder**
densed cream of	⅓ **cup sliced almonds**
chicken soup	

Place opened packages of broccoli on paper toweling in microwave oven. Micro-cook on 100% (*HIGH*) 5 to 7 minutes or until defrosted. Drain well. In a 2-quart casserole combine broccoli, chicken or turkey, soup, mayonnaise, wine, milk, garlic powder, ½ teaspoon *salt,* and ⅛ teaspoon *pepper*. Micro-cook, uncovered, on 100% (*HIGH*) 5 minutes, stirring after 3 minutes. Stir; sprinkle with almonds. Reduce power to 50% (*MEDIUM*). Micro-cook, uncovered, 5 to 7 minutes or until heated through, rotating once. Makes 6 servings.

HOT POULTRY SALAD

1 **cup sliced celery**	1 **tablespoon lemon juice**
¼ **cup chopped onion**	1 **teaspoon sugar**
2 **cups cubed cooked**	1 **teaspoon dry mustard**
chicken *or* **turkey**	1 **1½-ounce can shoestring**
⅔ **cup mayonnaise**	**potatoes**

In a 1½-quart casserole combine celery, onion, and 2 tablespoons *water*. Micro-cook, covered, on 100% (*HIGH*) 2½ to 3 minutes or until crisp-tender. Drain. Stir in chicken or turkey. Micro-cook, uncovered, on 100% (*HIGH*) 2 minutes or until chicken is heated through. Combine mayonnaise, lemon juice, sugar, mustard, ¼ teaspoon *salt,* and dash *pepper*. Add to chicken and vegetables; stir in *half* of the potatoes. Micro-cook, uncovered, on 100% (*HIGH*) 1 minute. Stir. Sprinkle remaining potatoes over top. Micro-cook, uncovered, on 100% (*HIGH*) 30 to 60 seconds or till heated through. Makes 4 servings.

Leftover Poultry

Cooked poultry for your favorite casseroles, salads, and sandwiches is minutes away with your microwave. Micro-cook chicken parts in a covered dish on 100% (HIGH) for 5½ to 7½ minutes per pound. Micro-cook a turkey hind quarter uncovered for 13 to 16 minutes per pound, starting on 100% (HIGH) for the first 10 minutes, then reducing power to 50% (MEDIUM) to finish. Turn chicken or turkey parts over after half the time.

VEGETABLES

Microwaved vegetables retain their vitamins and fresh color, flavor, and texture. In this section, you'll find new recipes for family favorites, colorful vegetable mixtures, and protein-rich combinations hearty enough to serve with a sandwich as a supper main dish.

SPINACH PUFF

1	10-ounce package frozen chopped spinach	Dash pepper
¼	cup butter *or* margarine	1 cup milk
¼	cup all-purpose flour	½ cup shredded cheddar cheese (2 ounces)
¾	teaspoon salt	4 egg yolks
¼	teaspoon dry mustard	4 egg whites
⅛	teaspoon paprika	¼ teaspoon cream of tartar
	Dash ground nutmeg	

Place package of spinach on paper toweling on floor of oven. Micro-cook on 100% (*HIGH*) 4 to 6 minutes or until defrosted. Drain well. Set aside. In a 2-quart casserole or bowl micro-cook butter or margarine, uncovered, on 100% (*HIGH*) 45 seconds to 1½ minutes or until melted. Blend in flour, salt, mustard, paprika, nutmeg, and pepper. Stir in milk. Micro-cook, uncovered, on 100% (*HIGH*) 4 to 6 minutes or until thickened, stirring after 2 minutes and then every minute. Stir in cheese until melted. Stir in spinach.

Beat egg yolks slightly. Slowly add to spinach mixture, stirring constantly. Set aside. In a large bowl beat egg whites with cream of tartar until soft peaks form. Gently fold into sauce mixture. Pour into an ungreased 8×1½- or 9×1½-inch round baking dish. Micro-cook, uncovered, on 30% (*MEDIUM-LOW*) 15 to 40 minutes or until just set in center, rotating dish 3 or 4 times as needed. Makes 6 to 8 servings.

ARTICHOKES WITH LEMON

2 **medium artichokes**	1 **teaspoon finely shredded**
¼ **cup water**	**lemon peel**
⅛ **teaspoon salt**	½ **teaspoon dried parsley**
1 **medium lemon**	**flakes**
¼ **cup butter *or* margarine**	½ **teaspoon snipped chives**
	Dash pepper

Cut 1-inch from top of artichokes and cut off stem close to base. Cut off sharp tips of outer leaves. Pull off any loose leaves. Place artichokes in an 8×8×2-inch baking dish. Add water and salt. Cut lemon into eight slices. Cut each slice in half. Arrange half of lemon slices in each artichoke, placing them cut side down between leaves.

Cover dish with vented plastic wrap. Micro-cook on 100% (*HIGH*) 9 to 15 minutes or until outer leaves come out with a slight pull, rotating dish a half-turn after half the cooking time. Set aside.

Place butter or margarine in a small dish, cover with waxed paper. Micro-cook on 100% (*HIGH*) 45 seconds to 1½ minutes or until melted. Stir in lemon peel, parsley flakes, chives, and pepper. Serve with artichokes. Makes 2 to 4 servings.

ASPARAGUS WITH SHRIMP SAUCE

1 **8-ounce package frozen**	⅛ **teaspoon pepper**
asparagus spears	**Dash cayenne**
1 **tablespoon water**	1 **cup milk**
2 **tablespoons butter *or***	1 **4½-ounce can tiny**
margarine	**shrimp, rinsed and**
2 **tablespoons all-purpose**	**drained**
flour	**Toast points**
½ **teaspoon dried parsley**	¼ **cup slivered almonds**
flakes	

In a 2-quart casserole micro-cook asparagus with water, covered, on 100% (*HIGH*) 8 to 10 minutes or until crisp-tender, rearranging spears after half the cooking time. Let stand while preparing sauce.

In a 4-cup measure micro-cook butter or margarine, uncovered, on 100% (*HIGH*) 30 to 60 seconds or until melted. Stir in flour, parsley flakes, pepper, and cayenne until smooth. Add milk, all at once, stirring constantly. Micro-cook, uncovered, on 100% (*HIGH*) 4 to 8 minutes or until thickened, stirring after the first 2 minutes and then every minute. Stir in shrimp.

Drain asparagus; arrange on toast points. Spoon sauce over asparagus spears and sprinkle with almonds. Micro-cook on 50% (*MEDIUM*) for 1 to 2 minutes or till heated through. Makes 2 servings.

BRUSSELS SPROUTS WITH WALNUTS

2 8-ounce packages frozen brussels sprouts	1 tablespoon milk
2 tablespoons water	2 tablespoons butter
½ of an 11-ounce can condensed cheddar cheese soup	3 tablespoons fine dry bread crumbs
	3 tablespoons chopped walnuts

In a 1½-quart casserole combine brussels sprouts and water; cover. Micro-cook on 100% (*HIGH*) 7 to 11 minutes or until fork-tender, stirring after half the cooking time. Drain. Mix in soup, milk, and dash *pepper*. Let stand while preparing topping.

For topping, in a small bowl micro-cook butter, uncovered, on 100% (*HIGH*) 30 to 50 seconds or until melted. Stir in bread crumbs and walnuts; sprinkle over brussels sprouts. Micro-cook, uncovered, on 100% (*HIGH*) 2 to 4 minutes or until thoroughly heated. Makes 4 to 6 servings.

THREE-BEAN DISH

½ pound ground beef	1 15½-ounce can garbanzo beans, drained
6 slices bacon, cut in eighths	¾ cup catsup
1 medium onion, chopped	½ cup packed brown sugar
1 clove garlic, minced	1 tablespoon vinegar
1 28-ounce can baked beans	1 tablespoon prepared mustard
1 16-ounce can lima beans, drained	

In a 3-quart casserole combine ground beef, bacon, onion, and garlic. Micro-cook, uncovered, on 100% (*HIGH*) 4 to 6 minutes or until ground beef and bacon are cooked (bacon will still be limp), stirring after half the cooking time. Drain.

Mix in beans, catsup, brown sugar, vinegar, mustard, and 1 teaspoon *salt*. Micro-cook, uncovered, on 100% (*HIGH*) 12 to 15 minutes or until hot, stirring after half the cooking time. Serves 6.

ORIENTAL MEDLEY

1 6-ounce package frozen pea pods	1 cup thinly sliced celery
1 tablespoon soy sauce	1 tablespoon butter *or* margarine, melted
1 tablespoon cornstarch	⅛ teaspoon ground ginger
1 8-ounce can sliced water chestnuts, drained	⅛ teaspoon paprika
	¼ cup cashews

Defrost pea pods in package on 100% (*HIGH*) 50 seconds or until pods separate easily. In a medium bowl stir soy sauce into cornstarch; stir in water chestnuts, celery, butter or margarine, ginger, and paprika. Let stand. Preheat a 10-inch browning dish on 100% (*HIGH*) 3 minutes. Add vegetable mixture and cashews. Micro-cook, uncovered, on 100% (*HIGH*) 3 to 5 minutes or until pea pods are crisp-tender, stirring after half the cooking time. Makes 6 servings.

Saving Leftover Soup

The remaining half can of cheese soup can be frozen in a small container. To defrost, micro-cook on 50% (MEDIUM) 3 minutes or until softened, stirring to break up after half the cooking time.

A One-Stir Stir-Fry

Vegetables micro-cooked in a pre-heated browning dish taste like the ones you prepare in a wok, but you stir them once, not constantly.

Italian Medley

How to Micro-cook Bacon for a Vegetable Garnish

Place bacon on 3 layers of paper toweling. Cover with paper toweling. Micro-cook on 100% (HIGH) 1½ to 2½ minutes. Let stand 3 minutes to crisp. Crumble.

CARROTS, BROCCOLI, CAULIFLOWER, AND MUSHROOMS

1 **cup carrots, cut into 2×¼-inch sticks**	2 **tablespoons grated Parmesan cheese**
2 **tablespoons water**	2 **slices bacon, cooked and crumbled (optional)**
2 **cups small to medium cauliflower flowerets**	
2 **cups small to medium broccoli buds**	1 **tablespoon butter or margarine**
2 **tablespoons water**	¼ **teaspoon salt**
1½ **cups sliced fresh mushrooms**	**Dash pepper**

In a 1½-quart casserole combine carrots and 2 tablespoons water; cover. Micro-cook on 100% (*HIGH*) 2 minutes. Add cauliflower, broccoli buds, and 2 tablespoons water; cover. Micro-cook on 100% (*HIGH*) 4 to 6 minutes or until almost cooked, stirring once during cooking. Add mushrooms; cover. Micro-cook on 100% (*HIGH*) 1 to 3 minutes or until mushrooms are tender. Drain.

Toss vegetables with cheese, bacon, butter or margarine, salt, and pepper. Makes 4 to 6 servings.

ITALIAN MEDLEY

2 cups zucchini sliced ¼-inch thick
1 small onion, thinly sliced and separated into rings
2 tablespoons water
1 medium tomato, cut into wedges

1 tablespoon butter
½ teaspoon dried parsley flakes
½ teaspoon lemon juice
¼ teaspoon salt
¼ teaspoon dried basil, crushed

In a 9-inch pie plate or 1½-quart casserole combine zucchini, onion, and water; cover. Micro-cook on 100% (*HIGH*) 2 to 4 minutes or until almost done. Add tomato wedges; cover. Micro-cook on 100% (*HIGH*) 1 to 2 minutes; drain. Gently stir in butter, parsley flakes, lemon juice, salt, and basil. Makes 4 servings.

RICE PILAF

1 10¾-ounce can condensed chicken broth
1 cup long grain rice
½ cup chopped green pepper
½ cup chopped onion
⅓ cup chopped celery
½ cup hot water
1 tablespoon dried parsley flakes

¼ teaspoon salt
¼ teaspoon dried marjoram, crushed
Dash pepper
¼ cup raisins
¼ cup chopped peanuts *or* cashews
1 tablespoon butter *or* margarine

In a 2-quart casserole combine chicken broth, rice, green pepper, onion, celery, water, parsley flakes, salt, marjoram, and pepper. Cover tightly with plastic wrap. Micro-cook on 100% (*HIGH*) for 5 minutes. Stir. Reduce power to 50% (*MEDIUM*). Micro-cook 13 to 18 minutes or till rice is tender and liquid is absorbed, stirring once. Stir in raisins, peanuts or cashews, and butter or margarine. Let stand, covered, 5 minutes. Makes 4 to 6 servings.

> ### Microwaving Raw Rice
>
> *Raw or converted long grain rice needs time to absorb liquid and tenderize. Start it on 100% (HIGH), then reduce the power to 50% (MEDIUM) so liquid will not cook away before the rice is tender.*

PEAS, ONION, MUSHROOMS, AND ALMONDS

1 small onion, chopped (½ cup)
1 tablespoon butter *or* margarine
3 cups frozen peas
1 10¾-ounce can condensed cream of mushroom soup

1 4-ounce can mushroom stems and pieces, drained
1 teaspoon lemon juice
½ teaspoon sugar
1 3-ounce can french-fried onions
¼ cup sliced almonds

In a 1½-quart casserole combine onion and butter or margarine. Micro-cook, uncovered, on 100% (*HIGH*) 1 to 2 minutes or until onion is tender. Stir in peas, soup, mushrooms, lemon juice, sugar, and *half* of the french-fried onions. Micro-cook, uncovered, on 100% (*HIGH*) 7 to 13 minutes or until peas are tender, stirring once during cooking. Stir. Sprinkle with remaining french-fried onions and the almonds. Micro-cook, uncovered, on 100% (*HIGH*) 2 minutes. Makes 6 servings.

Cutting Squash

If winter squash is difficult to cut, micro-cook on 100% (HIGH) for 1 to 2 minutes. Then halve and scoop out seeds.

STUFFED ACORN SQUASH

2 **small to medium acorn squash**	2 **tablespoons brown sugar**
2 **medium cooking apples, peeled and chopped (2 cups)**	2 **teaspoons all-purpose flour**
	⅛ **teaspoon ground cinnamon**
2 **Polish sausages, halved lengthwise and cut into ¼-inch slices (8 ounces total)**	**Dash ground nutmeg**
	1 **teaspoon butter *or* margarine**

Cut squash in half lengthwise. Remove seeds and fibrous membranes. Place squash, cut side down, in a 12×7½×2-inch baking dish. Cover with clear plastic wrap; vent. Micro-cook on 100% (*HIGH*) 10 to 15 minutes or just till tender, rotating dish a half-turn after 5 minutes. Let stand while preparing filling.

For filling, in a 1½-quart casserole combine apples, sausages, brown sugar, flour, cinnamon, and nutmeg. Micro-cook, covered, on 100% (*HIGH*) 4 to 6 minutes or until apples are tender, stirring after 2 minutes. Turn squash halves cut side up. Spread evenly with butter or margarine. Spoon ¼ of the filling into each half. Micro-cook, uncovered, on 100% (*HIGH*) 1 to 2 minutes or till heated through. Makes 4 servings.

BARLEY-VEGETABLE STEW

4 **medium carrots, thinly sliced (2 cups)**	1 **10¾-ounce can condensed chicken broth**
2 **medium potatoes, peeled and cut into ½-inch cubes (2 cups)**	½ **cup pearl barley**
	1 **bay leaf**
2 **stalks celery, sliced (1 cup)**	1 **teaspoon salt**
	1 **teaspoon dried parsley flakes**
1 **medium onion, thinly sliced (½ cup)**	½ **teaspoon dried basil, crushed**
1 **16-ounce can tomatoes**	⅛ **teaspoon pepper**
1 **15-ounce can black-eyed peas, drained**	⅛ **teaspoon garlic powder**
½ **of a 10-ounce package frozen cut green beans**	2 **tablespoons all-purpose flour**
1¾ **cups hot water**	½ **cup cold water**

In a 4- to 5-quart casserole combine carrots, potatoes, celery, onion, tomatoes, peas, beans, 1¾ cups hot water, broth, barley, bay leaf, salt, parsley, basil, pepper, and garlic powder. Micro-cook, covered, on 100% (*HIGH*) 25 minutes.

Blend flour with ¼ *cup* cold water; stir into stew with remaining ¼ cup water. Micro-cook, uncovered, on 100% (*HIGH*) 20 to 30 minutes or until barley and vegetables are tender, stirring once during cooking. Remove bay leaf. Makes 10 to 12 servings.

SWEET POTATO CASSEROLE

2 tablespoons butter *or* margarine	**¼ teaspoon ground cinnamon**
1 23-ounce can sweet potatoes, drained	**⅛ teaspoon ground nutmeg**
3 tablespoons maple-flavored syrup	**⅛ teaspoon salt**
	Dash ground cloves
1 tablespoon milk	**½ cup tiny marshmallows**
	¼ cup chopped pecans

In a small nonmetal mixer bowl micro-cook butter or margarine on 100% (*HIGH*) 40 to 60 seconds or until melted; add potatoes and beat with electric mixer till smooth. Stir syrup, milk, cinnamon, nutmeg, salt, and cloves into potatoes. Spoon into a 1-quart casserole. Micro-cook, uncovered, on 100% (*HIGH*) 4 to 8 minutes or until thoroughly heated. Sprinkle marshmallows and pecans over top. Micro-cook, uncovered, on 100% (*HIGH*) 1 to 1½ minutes or until marshmallows are softened. Makes 4 servings.

WHIPPED POTATO PUFF WITH CHEESE SAUCE

4 medium potatoes, peeled and quartered (4 cups)	**¼ cup finely crushed cheese-flavored crackers**
⅔ cup milk	
2 tablespoons butter *or* margarine	**2 tablespoons butter *or* margarine**
Dash cayenne	**2 tablespoons all-purpose flour**
3 egg yolks	
1 cup dairy sour cream	**½ teaspoon dry mustard**
1 3-ounce can sliced mushrooms, drained	**1 cup milk**
3 egg whites	**½ cup shredded cheddar cheese**
¼ teaspoon cream of tartar	

In a 2-quart casserole combine potatoes, ¼ cup *water*, and ½ teaspoon *salt*. Micro-cook, covered, on 100% (*HIGH*) 10 to 12 minutes or until tender. Drain. Mash potatoes with ⅔ cup milk, 2 tablespoons butter or margarine, cayenne, 1 teaspoon *salt*, and ⅛ teaspoon *pepper* until smooth. Let cool to lukewarm.

Beat egg yolks and sour cream into potatoes. Stir in mushrooms. Beat egg whites with cream of tartar until soft peaks form. Fold into potato mixture. Pour into a 1½- to 2-quart soufflé dish or casserole.

Micro-cook, uncovered, on 100% (*HIGH*) 2 minutes. Reduce power to 50% (*MEDIUM*). Micro-cook, uncovered, 9 to 16 minutes or until edges of puff are firm and hot in center (center will remain creamy). Sprinkle with cracker crumbs. Cover; set aside.

For sauce, in a 1-quart bowl micro-cook 2 tablespoons butter or margarine, uncovered, on 100% (*HIGH*) 40 to 60 seconds or until melted. Stir in flour, mustard, ¼ teaspoon *salt*, and ⅛ teaspoon *pepper*. Stir in 1 cup milk. Micro-cook, uncovered, on 100% (*HIGH*) 5 to 8 minutes or until thickened, stirring after first 2 minutes and then every minute. Stir in cheese until smooth. Serve with potato puff. Makes 6 servings.

Traditional Favorite, Microwave Speed

This popular casserole bakes about 30 minutes conventionally, but is ready in less than 10 minutes of microwaving. Add the marshmallows after the dish is heated through; they puff and soften rapidly.

FRESH VEGETABLES

Vegetable	Power Level	Cooking Time	Standing Time	Method
Acorn Squash, halved & seeded				
(1-1½ pounds)	100% (HIGH)	5½-8 min.	3-5 min.	Place in a tightly covered 10×6-inch dish; rotate once.
(2-2½ pounds)	100% (HIGH)	13-16 min.	3-5 min.	Place in a tightly covered 10×6-inch dish; rotate once.
Asparagus *(1 pound)*	100% (HIGH)	5½-9 min.	3-5 min.	Place in a tightly covered 12×7½×2-inch dish with 2 tablespoons water; rotate once.
Broccoli *(1½ pounds)*	100% (HIGH)	8-12 min.	3-5 min.	Cut off tough part of stalks. Cut stalks lengthwise into uniform spears, following branching lines. Place in a tightly covered 12×7½×2-inch dish with ¼ cup water; rotate once.
Brussels Sprouts *(4 cups, cleaned)*	100% (HIGH)	4-8 min.	3 min.	Place in a tightly covered 1½-quart casserole with ¼ cup water; stir once.
Cabbage *(1 pound)*	100% (HIGH)	7½-13½ min.	3 min.	Cut into ¼-inch-wide shreds. Place in a tightly covered 1½-quart casserole with 2 tablespoons water; stir once.
Carrots *(2 cups)*	100% (HIGH)	4½-6½ min.	3 min.	Cut into ⅛-inch-thick slices. Place in a 1-quart casserole with 2 tablespoons water; stir once.
Cauliflower *(1-pound head)*	100% (HIGH)	5½-7½ min.	3 min.	Wrap in vented clear plastic wrap; place on dinner plate. Turn over after 3 minutes.
Cauliflower flowerets *(2 cups)*	100% (HIGH)	5-7 min.	3 min.	Place in a tightly covered medium bowl with 2 tablespoons water; stir once.
Corn on the Cob *(7-8 ounces each)* 4 ears	100% (HIGH)	12-16 min.	3-5 min.	Place in a tightly covered 12×7½×2-inch casserole with 2 tablespoons water; rotate once.
Green Beans, Wax Beans *(1 pound)*	100% (HIGH)	7-13½ min.	3 min.	Cut into 1½-inch pieces. Place in a tightly covered 1½-quart casserole with ¼ cup water; stir once.
Green Peas *(2 cups, shelled)*	100% (HIGH)	5-8 min.	3 min.	Place in a tightly covered 1-quart casserole with ¼ cup water; stir once.

Potatoes, Medium Baking
(5-7 ounces each)

1 potato	100% (HIGH)	3-5 min.	5 min.	Wash, prick, and place in oven on paper
2 potatoes	100% (HIGH)	6-8 min.	5 min.	toweling. When cooking two or more,
4 potatoes	100% (HIGH)	10½-12½ min.	5 min.	rearrange once.

Spinach
(1 pound, cleaned)

	100% (HIGH)	5-8 min.	3 min.	Place in a tightly covered 3-quart casserole; stir once.

Sweet Potatoes or Yams
(5-7 ounces each)

1 potato	100% (HIGH)	3-5 min.	3 min.	Wash, prick, and place in oven on paper
2 potatoes	100% (HIGH)	5-9 min.	3 min.	toweling. When cooking two or more,
4 potatoes	100% (HIGH)	8-13 min.	3 min.	rearrange once.

Zucchini
(2 cups)

	100% (HIGH)	2½-6½ min.	3 min.	Cut into ⅛-inch-thick slices. Place in a tightly covered 1-quart casserole; stir once.

FROZEN VEGETABLES (10-ounce package, unless otherwise stated)

Cook vegetables in a 1-quart casserole with 2 tablespoons water; stir once. Cover while standing.

Vegetable	Power Level	Cooking Time	Standing Time
Asparagus	100% (HIGH)	5-7 min.	3 min.
Broccoli	100% (HIGH)	5-7 min.	3 min.
Brussels Sprouts	100% (HIGH)	5-7 min.	3 min.
Cauliflower	100% (HIGH)	5-7 min.	3 min.
Corn on the Cob *(2 small ears)*	100% (HIGH)	5½-7½ min.	3 min.
Cut Green Beans *(9-ounce package)*	100% (HIGH)	4-7 min.	3 min.
Green Peas	100% (HIGH)	4-6 min.	3 min.
Leaf or Chopped Spinach	100% (HIGH)	7-9 min.	3 min.
Lima Beans	100% (HIGH)	4-7 min.	3 min.
Mixed Vegetables	100% (HIGH)	4-6 min.	3 min.
Sliced Carrots *(2 cups)*	100% (HIGH)	4-7 min.	3 min.
Whole Kernel Corn	100% (HIGH)	4-6 min.	3 min.

DESSERTS

What's for dessert? When you use a microwave oven, there's always time to make dessert. Try these microwave-modern versions of family favorites and company pleasers.

HAWAIIAN CREAM TORTE

1 cup all-purpose flour	1 cup whipping cream
⅔ cup granulated sugar	2 tablespoons powdered
1¼ teaspoons baking	sugar
powder	½ teaspoon almond *or* rum
½ teaspoon salt	extract
½ teaspoon vanilla	¼ cup pineapple preserves
2 eggs	2 teaspoons lemon juice
⅓ cup milk	½ cup flaked coconut
⅓ cup shortening	

For cake, in a mixer bowl combine flour, granulated sugar, baking powder, salt, and vanilla. Add eggs, milk, and shortening. Beat at low speed of electric mixer till mixed; beat at medium speed 2 minutes, scraping bowl occasionally. Spread batter in an 8 × 1½-inch waxed-paper-lined round cake dish. Micro-cook, uncovered, on 50% (*MEDIUM*) 6 minutes, rotating a quarter-turn every 2 minutes. Increase power to 100% (*HIGH*). Micro-cook, uncovered, 1½ to 5 minutes or until done. Cool on a wire rack 5 to 10 minutes. Remove from pan; cool thoroughly on rack. Slice cooled cake horizontally to make two thin layers. Place bottom layer on serving plate. Set aside.

For topping, beat whipping cream, powdered sugar, and almond or rum extract until stiff peaks form. In a 1-cup measure combine preserves and lemon juice. Spread on bottom cake layer. Top with ¼ of whipped cream mixture. Top with the remaining cake layer. Top with ⅓ of the remaining whipped cream mixture. Spread remainder of whipped cream on sides. Sprinkle with coconut. Refrigerate until served. Makes 8 servings.

GINGERBREAD UPSIDE-DOWN CAKE

1 **8¼-ounce can pineapple slices**	¼ **teaspoon ground cinnamon**
2 **tablespoons butter** *or* **margarine**	1· **14½-ounce package gingerbread mix**
¼ **cup packed brown sugar**	½ **cup shredded carrot**

Drain pineapple slices, reserving 1 tablespoon of the syrup. In an 8×8×2-inch baking dish micro-cook butter or margarine on 100% (*HIGH*) 30 seconds. Stir the reserved syrup, brown sugar, and cinnamon into the butter. Cut pineapple slices in half; arrange in bottom of baking dish. Prepare gingerbread mix according to package directions. Stir in carrot. Starting from outside of pan and working in, carefully pour batter evenly over pineapple mixture in pan. Micro-cook, uncovered, on 100% (*HIGH*) 11 to 12 minutes, giving dish a quarter-turn every 3 minutes. Let cake stand 1 to 2 minutes before inverting onto a serving platter. Serve cake warm with whipped cream, if desired. Makes 8 to 10 servings.

RHUBARB STREUSEL CAKE

3 **tablespoons brown sugar**	½ **teaspoon salt**
2 **tablespoons all-purpose flour**	½ **teaspoon ground cinnamon**
½ **teaspoon ground cinnamon**	¼ **teaspoon ground nutmeg**
2 **tablespoons butter** *or* **margarine**	⅛ **teaspoon ground cloves**
¼ **cup chopped nuts**	⅓ **cup shortening**
¾ **cup all-purpose flour**	2 **eggs**
⅔ **cup granulated sugar**	¼ **cup milk**
½ **teaspoon baking soda**	1 **cup rhubarb, cut into ½-inch pieces***
	Whipping cream, whipped

In a small bowl combine brown sugar, 2 tablespoons flour, and ½ teaspoon cinnamon; cut in butter or margarine until crumbly. Stir in nuts; set aside.

In a small mixer bowl combine ¾ cup flour, granulated sugar, baking soda, salt, ½ teaspoon cinnamon, nutmeg, and cloves. Add shortening, eggs, and milk. Blend at low speed of electric mixer, then beat at medium speed 2 minutes, scraping bowl occasionally. Stir in rhubarb. Spread batter in an 8×1½-inch round baking dish. Micro-cook, uncovered, on 50% (*MEDIUM*) 10½ to 16½ minutes or until top of cake is no longer wet, rotating dish a half-turn 2 or 3 times. (Slight moistness may remain but will cook after cake is removed from oven.) Sprinkle with brown sugar mixture. Micro-cook, uncovered, on 100% (*HIGH*) 30 seconds. Let stand on counter 5 to 10 minutes. Serve cake warm or cool with whipped cream. Makes 1 cake.

***Note:** If using frozen rhubarb, thaw and drain thoroughly.

INDIVIDUAL CUSTARDS

2 **cups milk**	1 **teaspoon vanilla**
4 **beaten eggs**	**Dash salt**
⅓ **cup sugar**	**Ground nutmeg**

In a 4-cup measure micro-cook milk on 100% (*HIGH*) 2½ to 4 minutes or until very hot but not boiling. Meanwhile, in a small mixing bowl combine beaten eggs, sugar, vanilla, and salt. Beat with a wire whisk until well blended. Gradually add hot milk to egg mixture, beating with wire whisk.

Divide mixture evenly between six 6-ounce custard cups. Sprinkle with nutmeg. Place custard cups in a 12×7½×2-inch baking dish. Pour ½ cup hot water around cups in baking dish. Cover dish with waxed paper.

Micro-cook on 100% (*HIGH*) 4½ minutes, giving dish a half-turn once. Shake each custard gently and remove any that are soft-set. Rearrange remaining custards. Micro-cook on 100% (*HIGH*) 30 seconds to 2½ minutes more, checking each custard for doneness every 30 seconds. (When only 1 or 2 custards are left, check every 15 seconds.) Let custards stand 15 to 20 minutes to finish cooking. Serve warm or chilled. Makes 6 servings.

CHERRY BERRY PIE

2 **pounds frozen unsweet-ened whole strawberries**	½ **teaspoon ground cinnamon**
1 **16-ounce can pitted dark sweet cherries**	2 **teaspoons lemon juice**
⅓ **cup sugar**	1 **micro-cooked 9-inch Pastry Shell (see recipe, page 90)**
3 **tablespoons cornstarch**	**Whipping cream, whipped**

In a large mixing bowl micro-cook strawberries, uncovered, on 100% (*HIGH*) 7 to 8½ minutes or until thawed and juicy, stirring once or twice. Drain strawberries thoroughly, reserving ½ cup juice. Drain cherries, reserving ¾ cup juice. For sauce, in another large mixing bowl combine reserved cherry syrup and reserved strawberry juice. Combine sugar, cornstarch, and cinnamon; stir into juice mixture. Stir in lemon juice. Micro-cook, uncovered, on 100% (*HIGH*) 4½ to 5½ minutes or until very thick, stirring 2 or 3 times. Cool 5 minutes, stirring occasionally.

Add cherries to strawberries in mixing bowl. Drain off any excess juice. Add sauce. Stir to coat fruit. Pour into pastry shell. Chill thoroughly. Top with whipped cream before serving.

Testing Custards for Doneness

Delicate custards continue to cook with internal heat after microwaving. To test for doneness, shake each custard gently. The center should quiver like soft-set gelatin. Remove custards as they are done. Test remaining ones frequently, as they will cook faster with less food in the oven.

Micro-Cook the Pie Shell First

Microwaved pastry is tender and flaky as long as the shell is cooked until it is dry and flaky before you add filling. An unbaked shell would absorb moisture from the filling and be underbaked and soggy.

PASTRY SHELL

½ cup shortening
1 tablespoon butter *or* margarine
1½ cups all-purpose flour
½ teaspoon salt
4 to 5 tablespoons cold water*

Cut shortening and butter into flour and salt until particles are the size of peas. Sprinkle with *1 tablespoon* cold water; toss with a fork. Push to side of bowl. Repeat with remaining water until all flour is moistened. Form into a ball. Flatten on a lightly floured surface. Roll dough from center to edge, forming a circle about 12 inches in diameter.

Fit pastry into a 9-inch pie plate; trim ½ inch beyond edge. Fold under and flute edge to form a high rim. Prick bottom and sides at ½-inch intervals with a fork. Prick continuously at bend of dish. Micro-cook, uncovered, on 100% (*HIGH*) 4 to 5 minutes or until crust is dry, rotating dish after half the cooking time. Makes one 9-inch pastry shell.

*Note: For a light yellow color, add 4 drops yellow food coloring.

DELUXE LEMON CREME PIE

1 cup sugar
3 tablespoons cornstarch
¼ teaspoon salt
1 cup water
1 tablespoon finely shredded lemon peel
⅓ cup lemon juice
3 beaten egg yolks
¼ cup butter *or* margarine
1 micro-cooked 9-inch Pastry Shell (see recipe, above)
1 cup whipping cream, whipped

For filling, in a 2-quart casserole combine sugar, cornstarch, and salt. Stir in water, lemon peel, and juice. Micro-cook, uncovered, on 100% (*HIGH*) 5 to 7 minutes or until very thick, stirring every 2 minutes. Stir a small amount of hot mixture into egg yolks, then return to hot mixture; blend well. Micro-cook, uncovered, on 50% (*MEDIUM*) 1 to 2 minutes to cook yolk. Stir in butter until melted. Cool slightly. Pour filling into shell; chill thoroughly. Spread whipped cream over top. Makes one 9-inch pie.

CHOCOLATE CHIP BARS

6 tablespoons butter *or* margarine
⅓ cup packed brown sugar
½ teaspoon vanilla
1 egg
⅔ cup all-purpose flour
¼ teaspoon baking soda
¼ teaspoon salt
½ cup semisweet chocolate pieces
¼ cup chopped nuts

In a medium mixing bowl cream butter or margarine, brown sugar, and vanilla; beat in egg. Stir together flour, soda, and salt; stir into creamed mixture. Spread in an 8×8×2-inch baking dish. Sprinkle with chocolate pieces and nuts. Set dish on an inverted microwave-safe saucer in oven. Micro-cook, uncovered, on 100% (*HIGH*) 3 to 4½ minutes or until the top is no longer wet and springs back to the touch, rotating dish a quarter-turn after 2 minutes. Cool. Cut into bars. Makes 25 bars.

Blueberry Cheesecake

BLUEBERRY CHEESECAKE

6 **tablespoons butter *or* margarine**	1 **tablespoon light corn syrup**
1¼ **cups finely crushed graham crackers**	2 **tablespoons water**
3 **tablespoons sugar**	2 **teaspoons lemon juice**
8 **ounces frozen unsweet-ened blueberries**	2 **8-ounce packages cream cheese**
2 **tablespoons sugar**	⅓ **cup milk**
1 **tablespoon cornstarch**	¼ **cup sugar**
	2 **eggs**

In an 8×1½- or 9×1½-inch round baking dish micro-cook butter or margarine, uncovered, on 100% (*HIGH*) 50 seconds to 1½ minutes or until melted. Stir in crushed graham crackers and 3 tablespoons sugar until well moistened. Press firmly against bottom and sides of dish. Micro-cook on 100% (*HIGH*) 1 to 3 minutes or until set, rotating once or twice. Set aside.

In a large bowl micro-cook blueberries, uncovered, on 100% (*HIGH*) 2 to 3 minutes or until thawed and juicy. Stir together 2 tablespoons sugar and the cornstarch; stir in corn syrup, water, and lemon juice. Mix into blueberries. Micro-cook, uncovered, on 100% (*HIGH*) 2 to 4 minutes or until thick, stirring twice. Set aside to cool.

In a small mixer bowl micro-cook cream cheese, uncovered, on 100% (*HIGH*) 30 seconds to 1 minute or until softened. Add milk, ¼ cup sugar, and eggs; beat at high speed of electric mixer until smooth. Pour cheese mixture evenly over crust.

Micro-cook, uncovered, on 50% (*MEDIUM*) 12 to 16 minutes or till center is almost set, rotating pan a quarter-turn every 4 minutes. Remove from oven. Cool. Spoon cooled blueberry mixture over cheesecake. Refrigerate until set. Makes 8 to 12 servings.

Microwaving Fruits

Fruits retain their fresh flavor and texture when microwaved because they cook rapidly in their own natural moisture. Both these desserts micro-cook in less than 15 minutes.

GLAZED BRANDIED PEARS Pictured on page 4

4 **pears, peeled and cored**	4 **drops red food coloring**
4 **cinnamon sticks (optional)**	**(optional)**
¼ **cup granulated sugar**	1 **teaspoon ground**
¼ **cup packed brown sugar**	**cinnamon**
1 **tablespoon cornstarch**	¼ **teaspoon ground nutmeg**
1 **tablespoon light corn**	⅛ **teaspoon ground cloves**
syrup	1 **tablespoon butter** *or*
⅓ **cup brandy**	**margarine**
½ **teaspoon vanilla**	

Slice ¼ inch off the bottom of each pear. Place each pear in a custard cup; place a cinnamon stick in the center of each pear, if desired. For sauce, in a 2-cup measure combine sugars and cornstarch. Add corn syrup, brandy, vanilla, food coloring, cinnamon, nutmeg, cloves, and butter or margarine; mix well. Micro-cook, uncovered, on 100% (*HIGH*) 2 minutes, stirring after 1 minute. Pour hot sauce equally over pears; cover each custard cup with clear plastic wrap. Set on waxed paper in microwave oven or in an 8×8×2-inch baking dish. Micro-cook, covered, on 100% (*HIGH*) 4 minutes, rotating after 2 minutes. Reduce power to 50% (*MEDIUM*). Micro-cook 2 to 8 minutes or until pears are just tender, rotating every 2 minutes. Let stand 10 minutes; serve warm. Makes 4 servings.

APPLE DESSERT

2 **tablespoons butter** *or*	½ **cup granulated sugar**
margarine	1 **tablespoon all-purpose**
½ **cup fine dry bread crumbs**	**flour**
2 **tablespoons chopped nuts**	½ **teaspoon ground**
or **coconut (optional)**	**cinnamon**
2 **tablespoons brown sugar**	**Vanilla ice cream**
5 **cups sliced, peeled apples**	
(about 7 apples)	

In a small bowl micro-cook butter or margarine on 100% (*HIGH*) 20 to 45 seconds or until melted. Stir in bread crumbs, nuts, and brown sugar until moistened. Set aside.

In a 1½-quart casserole combine apples, sugar, flour, and cinnamon. Micro-cook, uncovered, on 100% (*HIGH*) 5 minutes, stirring once during cooking. Stir again; top with bread crumb mixture. Micro-cook, uncovered, on 100% (*HIGH*) 4 to 9½ minutes or until fruit in center is tender, rotating dish once during cooking. Serve dessert warm or chilled with ice cream. Makes 4 to 6 servings.

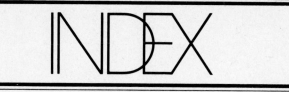